BOOK REVIEWS FOR

AN INVESTIGATION AND STUDY OF THE WHITE PEOPLE OF and
AMERICA AND WESTERN EUROPE

MIDWEST BOOK REVIEW

Impressively well written, exceptionally and effectively organized and presented, it is thoughtful and thought-provoking. *An Investigation and Study of the White People of America and Western Europe should be a part of every community and academic library.*
- James A. Cox, Editor-in-Chief, *Midwest Book Review; Small Press Bookwatch - The African American Studies Shelf.*

****

Often when a White reviewer reviews books about African American history they make the same mistake as the Kirkus Book Reviewer has in thinking that White Western European and White American extermination, slavery, racism, segregation and the brutal colonization of Africans, African Americans, Native Americans, Native South Americans, India, the Middle East, Native Australians and other people of color throughout the world, is as this reviewer states, "an exaggeration", and they tend to dwell more on the evils of the American ghettos and projects and find ways to excuse White Western European and White American capitalism, greed and racism as the prime problems for the destruction of tens of millions of African Americans living in our American cities. Although this reviewer has at least found the balls to say, *"my rambling exposition of the history of slavery and racism, contains much truth".*
- Tony Rose

KIRKUS BOOK REVIEW

White racism, slavery, and ongoing bigotry are to blame for the problems of black America, as well as the author's violent youth, according to this manifesto and accompanying memoir. Rose, a publisher and former record producer, opens his book with an essay. *Its subjects include the sins of white people against Africans, surveying the horrors of the Middle Passage; the violation of slave women by white owners in the American South and the brutalization and emasculation of black men;* the drug trade in black communities, which he contends is organized by the U.S. government; police killings; and the ingrained racism of some 70 percent of whites. **Rose's rambling exposition of the history of slavery and racism, contains much truth.** However, it also contains exaggeration and stereotyping of people of European descent, **whom he characterizes as** *"primitive, barbaric, vicious white monkeys [who] descended with the horrors of their psychotic desires and thirst for blood, rape and death on so-called uncivilized African and people of color throughout the world."* He calls for reparations, and urges African-American youngsters to avoid drugs and crime and get an education; less constructively, he suggests that **"whenever we meet or see a white man we should all just spit on him** for the death of our millions of ancestors." *However, his prose is vigorous and vivid, and sometimes pungent, scabrous, and sexually graphic.* It leaves a lasting impression of the chaos, deprivation, and psychic ravages of the ghetto, but also gives readers a more nuanced, three-dimensional view of its social life and its people. **A sometimes-distorted and sometimes-revealing portrait of a nightmarish United States.**
- David Rapp, Kirkus Book Review

****

KAM WILLIAMS BOOK REVIEW

A 200+ page blistering attack on the 70% of White America that remains ostensibly indifferent to the country's shameful legacy of slavery, segregation and institutional racism. For, their destructive by-products exact a continuing toll as evidenced in the African-American masses' ongoing suffering in squalor due to a seemingly-irreversible cultural collapse. *A searing indictment of the United States as a racist society. "A MUST READ".*
- Kam Williams, *International Music, Film, and Book Reviewer, Baret News Syndicate.*

****

You must read An Investigation and Study of the White People of America and Western Europe...One thing that stood out to me was that a lot of behavior that we see among blacks, especially in ghettos and low income neighborhoods, stems from the evil that was done to us by white people for hundreds of years, including the years preceding the trans-Atlantic slave trade. That is one of the hard truths in this book, among many others. I was impressed with how Mr. Rose laid out his theses on various topics throughout the book. After finishing this book, I was left to re-examine my own thought processes regarding our people and also the white diaspora. I am guilty of prejudging without understanding pathology. *This book has given me a better understanding of history and how history has affected and infected generations of our society at large. It's truly and eye-opening read.*
 - Teresa Price - Amazon.com

****

When a White child commits atrocities in America it must be because he fell through the cracks and didn't get the mental help he so deserved. *When a Black child commits horrific crimes and murder, it's because he's black and by birth is a brutal animal and gets life and forever in jail, where his or her abuse and life continues to be one long night in hell,"* an excerpt from The Investigation and Study of the White People of America and Western Europe'. This book offers an understanding to the evils of ghetto life without accepting its destruction to the human soul. *Read the book over and over again if you can take the truth.*
- Deborah Rene', book critic, ghost writer, and entertainment editor.

****

An Investigation and Study of the White People of America and Western Europe *is a **must read** for everyone*
- Lynette McMillon, President, The Tushe Group, Public Relations.

****

After the recent incidents in Ferguson, New York, Baltimore, Charleston and the birth of the Black Lives Matter Movement, **An Investigation and Study of the White People of America and Western Europe** *is timely and right on point.* ***A must read.***
- Kendall A. Minter, Esq. Legendary Entertainment Attorney and Author of, *Understanding and Negotiating 360 Ancillary Rights Deals:* An Artists Guide to Negotiating 360 Record Deals.

****

I highly, highly, recommend this book!
- Maggie Linton, *The Maggie Linton Show, Sirius XM Radio, Channel 126.*
****

Took my breathe away!
- Terrie Williams, *Founder/President of the Terrie Williams Agency, Mental Health Advocate/Author of Black Pain: It Just Looks Like We're Not Hurting.*

****

Congratulations Tony. ***This is an outstanding literary accomplishment.***
- Earl Cobb, CEO and Managing Partner, Richer Life, LLC, Author, *The Leadership Advantage. Do More. Lead More. Earn More.*, co-host of "*Living a Richer Life - Life Changing Talk Radio*".

****

America is indebted to Mr. Rose for writing this biting, brutally-honest, wake-up call masterpiece.
- Roland Barksdale-Hall, Librarian, Black Caucus of the American Library Association (BCALA), Community Activist and Author of *The African American Family's Guide to Tracing Our Roots: Healing, Understanding and Restoring Our Families*

****

Tony Rose has provided a unique look and report on the white people of America and Western Europe. His perspective is real and should be read by everyone who wants to know the "real" history.
- Farrell Chiles, Activist and Author of *As BIG As It Gets: A Chairman of the Board's Rise and Tenure at the Top - Lessons in Leadership and African American Warrant Officers...In Service To Our Country.*

I have personally and repeatedly witnessed the extraordinary genius of Tony Rose; however, his written words in *An Investigation and Study of the White People of America and Western Europe* have outdone all accountings that I have seen written by anyone in an attempt to outline a true and thorough history of man's evolution and his ancestry as it crossed the color lines and evolved throughout the world. *Rose has not only detailed the foundation of the evolution, but he has brought the reader into a three-dimensional world. If you are interested in knowing the Truth about the white man's effect on the Black man's slave mentality and the chains that have not been broken because of centuries of degradation which began in the slave ships and still exists to this day,* **READ THIS BOOK!**
- Yvonne Rose, *Director of Quality Press, Associate Publisher, Amber Communications Group, Inc., Author, Ageless Beauty,* - www.qualitypress.info - www.amberbooks.com

****

An Investigation and Study of the White People of America and Western Europe proves to be a very timely book, as it addresses the epidemic of shootings of unarmed blacks like Trayvon Martin, Jordan Davis and now the nine Charleston churchgoers by cowardly whites. The author points out that *"the weak white coward is not interested in going up against the real black gangster, they know the difference; but, they use the real black gangster as their excuse" for killing the innocent and the defenseless.*
- Troy Johnson, *Founder and Webmaster of the African American Literature Book Club* (AALBC.com)

****

Tony, My thanks to you. I am halfway through your latest book *that I truly believe that everyone of African American and White descent needs to read.*
- Marc Medley, *Host of the Reading Circle Radio Show on WPSC 88.7, Wayne New Jersey.*

****

Tony, I got the book last night. Up reading it till 3:00am. **_High powered and rapid_** machine gun fire!!! **_TOTALLY ENGROSSING. An Investigation and Study of the White People of America and Western Europe is a brilliantly written book and will most certainly be a 21st Century Classic_**
- Rod Ambrose, *Prevention Education Coordinator, City of Phoenix Parks and Recreation @ South Phoenix Youth Center, BRAVE Project Office*

****

"An Investigation and Study of the White People of America and Western Europe by Tony Rose, **_is a book that should be required reading in America's public schools and every College and University. A must read book!_** I found this book to be a source of reference regarding the development and tragedy of the journey of Africans to America.
– Jim Lopes, *Attorney and Law Professor, University of Massachusetts – Boston Campus*

****

This is an amazing and interesting book. And, with everything happening in America today, is especially important. I recommend it highly and think it will be of interest to readers around the world.
– Evelyn Lee, Global Rights, Literary Agent

AN INVESTIGATION AND STUDY OF THE WHITE PEOPLE OF AMERICA AND WESTERN EUROPE

BY TONY ROSE

AMBER BOOKS

Publisher's Note

The Publisher and Author shall have neither liability nor responsibility to any person or organization with respect to any loss or damage caused or alleged to be caused directly or indirectly by the information contained in this book. The purpose of this book is to educate, entertain and stimulate. This book is sold with the understanding that the Publisher and Author are not involved in offering legal, medical or psychological services. If any assistance is required, the services of a competent professional should be sought.

Copyright 2016 © by Tony Rose
Paperback ISBN #: 978-1-937269-48-7
eBook ISBN #: 978-1-937269-49-4

Library of Congress Cataloging-in-Publication Data

Names: Rose, Tony, 1953- author.
Title: An investigation and study of the White people of America and Western
Europe / by Tony Rose.
Description: Phoenix, AZ : Amber Books, [2016]
Identifiers: LCCN 2016010877 | ISBN 9781937269487 (pbk.)
Subjects: LCSH: European Americans--Race identity. | Whites--United States. |
Whites--Europe. | Racism--United States. | Racism--Europe. | United
States--Race relations. | Europe--Race relations.
Classification: LCC E184.E95 R68 2016 | DDC 305.800973--dc23
LC record available at http://lccn.loc.gov/2016010877

CONTENTS

ABOUT THE BOOK

INTRODUCTION... 1

AN INVESTIGATION AND STUDY OF DONALD TRUMP AND THE "WHITE MAN"

The Black and White Race in America 5
What is Wrong with White People 9
How Black Children are Seen by White Americans 13

**AN INVESTIGATION AND STUDY OF THE
WHITE PEOPLE OF AMERICA AND WESTERN EUROPE**

VOLUME ONE

THE INVESTIGATION

Chapter
1. I Pledge Allegiance to the Flag... 17
2. Spit on White People.. 21
3. Starving, Stinking and Raped 31
4. White Oppression and Terrorism 35
5. White Men, Sex, and Slaves 37
6. Sub Humans or Super Humans.. 45
7. Under Siege in Black America 55

AN INVESTIGATION AND STUDY OF THE WHITE PEOPLE OF AMERICA AND WESTERN EUROPE

VOLUME TWO

THE STUDY AND ORIGINS OF RACISM

Chapter
1. White Evolution... 61
2. White Death, Destruction and Enslavement 67
3. Warrior 71
4. Ugly White Ghosts.. 75

AN INVESTIGATION AND STUDY OF THE WHITE PEOPLE OF AMERICA AND WESTERN EUROPE

VOLUME THREE

AN INVESTIGATION AND STUDY OF BLACK PEOPLE .... POOR, BLACK AND GHETTOIZED

Chapter
1. The Black Community and Post-Traumatic Stress Disorder..... 79
2. Slave and Segregation Reparations.. 87
3. Black People and Slave Reparations 91
4. Black Wall Street 97
5. Slavery in the United States of America 99
6. Tarzan and Jane - Africa-Before Slavery 101
7. Black Lives Matter- The Killing of Black Men, Women and
    Children in America... 105

About the Author 139

ABOUT THE BOOK

The true and detailed story and history of the atrocities and horrors of what the White people of America and Western Europe did to West Africa, Africa, and its people for over five hundred years and the destruction of generations of hundreds and hundreds of millions of Africans, including African Americans in America and those of African descent around the world, has never really been told.

Who these White people were; What they were; Where they came from; What made the White people of Western Europe and America go crazy and have a blood lust and hatred for Africans, Africa, African Americans and people of African descent, to enslave, colonize and subjugate them for over five hundred years has never been told. UNTIL NOW!

INTRODUCTION

AN INVESTIGATION OF DONALD TRUMP AND "THE WHITE MAN"

Every person and country of color in the entire world hates the name, "The White Man". Every person and country of color hates "The White Man". Whenever "The White Man" has gone into countries of color, he has brought death, disease, rape, murder, massacres, prostitution, lies, stealing, enslavement, extinction, land theft, terrorism, his white Jesus religion, and much, much worse.

"The White Man" is a ridiculous, ignorant, dangerous and murderous person who doesn't know that everyone in the world laughs at his need for greed, world conquest and power. While all the time, dragging around the world his white, blonde, blue eyed Jesus. Praying to a white Jesus and a white God, when everyone knows that Jesus was a first century Hebrew from Judea, a Middle Easterner Levantine, who was a man of "brown complexion and lank, wooly hair", and that God who is everywhere and everything has no color. Yet "The White Man" will fight, kill and die for this ignorant, laughable belief and pray to a God and Jesus he thinks is in his white image.

Africans in Africa and African Americans in the United States of America especially hate the name, "The White Man", and especially hate "The White Man" and "The White Man" knows why. That's why "The White Man" of America and Western Europe lives in fear, hate and distrust of African Americans and people of color throughout the world.

For hundreds of years, Black people have lived with so much terror, terrorism and racism from "The White Man" in the United States of America, that the World Trade Center, 9/11, although horrific, was nothing in comparison to the terror that has been imposed by "The White Man" on our African forefathers and African Americans throughout the history of America.

The countries and people of color in the Middle East, Asia, South East Asia, Africa, India, the South Pacific, the Caribbean, the Native People of North and South America, the Aborigines of Australia, New Zealand, New Guinea, the Eskimos or Inuit people, the Hawaiian Islands, all hate the name "The White Man" and all hate "The White Man" who came to their countries with their wars, death, disease, racism and prejudice, lies, terrorism, religion, guns and weapons and pillaged, raped, enslaved, murdered, belittled their culture and stole their land.

I've been told that a lot of younger "White Men" don't know, don't understand what all the commotion is about in America with Black Lives Matter and around the world. Their history books in high school tell them that "The White Man" is privileged and powerful and has only brought good and heroic values to the world, and that the world that should love them, is just jealous of them.

They don't seem to understand why Black Lives Matter in America and what that is about. Well don't worry! This book will tell you why and what your father, your grandfather, your great-grandfather, your great-great grandfather, your great-great-great grandfather, and so on did to Native Americans, Africans and African Americans in Africa, the United States of America, Western Europe and people of color throughout the world.

This book will tell you why "The White Man" should cleanse himself and remove the stigma, stain, horror and disgrace of his name "The White Man" forever, into perpetuity, by beginning the process of calling himself what he is, a "European American Man". But, he won't because what "The White Man" name represents to him is power and white privilege over the Black and colored masses of the world.

As I was watching "The White Man" of America cry over the two thousand nine hundred and seventy-seven people killed at the World Trade Center, the one hundred and thirty people killed in Paris and the fourteen people killed in San Bernardino...

I was wondering if "The White Man" had cried over the hundreds and hundreds and hundreds of millions of African and African Americans he terrorized, enslaved, brutally killed, raped, murdered, pillaged, stole from, segregated, red-lined, ghettoized, performed institutional racism and intergenerational poverty on for over five hundred years, emotionally and physically destroying a whole culture.

2

I wondered did "The White Man" cry for the destroyed families and the mass selling of tens of millions of brutally whipped, beaten and raped Black Slaves in America.

I wondered did "The White Man" cry when he watched his government of the United States of America through acts of Congress parcel out and give millions and millions and millions of acres of land, free and superior education, agriculture and subsidies in the north, south, West and the Midwest to its white peasants and immigrants from Europe. Underwriting "The White Man" of America, with bank loans and an economic floor plan that lasts to this day, while giving nothing, absolutely nothing to its poor Black masses, except ghettos, projects and prison. Did you cry then?

Donald Trump, currently running for President of the United States of America, is the epitome of "The White Man's", white privilege and power in America. He is a throwback to every "White Man" who terrorized, demoralized, massacred, enslaved, raped, abused, and destroyed every Native American and African American in America.

He is what every "White Man" in America wants to be again. They, "The White Man", want America back so that they are free to keep all the colored people in their place. Free to be cruel harbingers of racism and prejudice. Free to take away every right, African Americans, Native Americans, Hispanic Americans and Asian Americans have lived, fought and died for in the tens of millions to get. Free to make America "The White Man's" domicile and round up, keep in our place, deport, destroy, keep jobless, poor, and begging to our so-called white masters and free to be politically incorrect.

These ignorant white people actually believe that Donald Trump cares about them and will make America white for "The White Man" again and when Donald J. Trump becomes the President of the White People of the United States of America, he damn well will do all that for "The White Man" and much, much more.

Donald Trump's 'Make America Great Again' slogan is a call to all racists and White Supremacists that he will take America back to the good old days of White oppression and terrorism. He the great Donald Trump will

'Make America White Again' for "The White Man".

Donald Trump is a wealthy, stupid, racist, greedy, evil, vicious, fat, ignorant, white bully, who has little regard for anybody, much less African Americans, and if elected will prey upon the weakest and poorest of men. He is a man born to great privilege and wealth, who is selling himself as a man of the white people of America. He is ready to be their leader, much as Hitler was ready to lead the white people of Germany.

He is saying what "The White Man" in America secretly wishes and wants, much like Hitler did in Germany, which is to dominate and control the world with his White Supremacist views and subjugate all the people of color in it.

"The White Man" has been responsible, since they crawled out of Greece and Rome, for wars that have brought suffering and death to countless trillions of people on earth. But, there was no greater mass murderer and serial killer than Adolph Hitler, who much like Donald Trump is preying on the lower middle class of America, Hitler preyed upon the lower middle class Aryan white people of Germany; telling them to take their country back, to make Germany great again, and led them to the slaughter and destruction of hundreds of millions of people all over the world, including themselves.

And now right here in America, Hitler has been reborn in the form of a wealthy white privileged, German immigrant scion, "White Man", named Donald Trump and the white media can't get enough of him, thinking he is just some harmless asshole.

If elected President of the United States of America he will bring more death, destruction, poverty, abuse and terrorism to untold millions of Black people and people of color in this country and around the world. This is secretly, under the covers, in the night, what "The White Man" of America really wants. He will keep his promise to "The White Man" and along with America's white police force, keep the Black ghettos and projects of America under siege and terrorized.

INTRODUCTION

****

THE BLACK AND WHITE RACE IN AMERICA

The words 'black race' and 'white race', have no meaning as do the words 'white and black people'. There is no such thing as the Black and White race, there is only the Human race and Human people.

The words 'black race' and 'white race' were words first used by Western European upper class scientists and noblemen during the 16th and 17th century to explain the differences between them and the Africans they were beginning to, with the use of guns and cannons, exploit and subjugate through force into chattel slavery

Thus, to differentiate themselves from these 'Africans' they came up with the language of race. The African being savage, inferior and sub-human and themselves superior, civilized and human. The African and the African American were sold to Europe and eventually to America as another race, the black race, sub-human and uncivilized; and the white race became in America civilized and human. The African had to be another species, another race, surely not related to Europeans and "The White Man".

To further define my point, you do not hear newscasters or politicians or people say, "The yellow race did that or the red race did that or the brown race did this. It's only used in context, still today, for the black race and the white race.

My recommendation is that the language of 'white race and black race' in the United States of America be changed to the African American Culture and the European American Culture, because as everyone knows there is only one race, the 'Human Race'… everything else is culture. The African Culture; The European Culture; The Asiatic Culture; The Hispanic Culture; and so on. And then you bring it down to specific countries and groupings of people. The Kenyan Culture; The English Culture; The Gambian Culture; The French Culture; The Irish Culture; and so on, and then to people; The African American Culture; The European American Culture. And that brings us to 'white and black people'…there is no such thing. The white people of America should cleanse themselves of the stain and disgrace of calling themselves "White People" and begin calling themselves "European Americans".

Before the enslavement of Africans in Western Europe and America began, there was no such thing as the white people of France, or the white people of England. There were only Frenchmen and Englishmen. Only in early America, after a time, did every person who was of European ancestry become known as a "White man" or woman, not Englishman, Frenchman or Dutchman; to again differentiate themselves, gain numbers and unify against the Africans and Native Americans. In America every person who was of African ancestry became known as a "negro", a "colored", a "black" or worse. One superior, the other inferior.

African Americans are not a minority in America. The word minority is used by the White people of America to make Black people and other American ethnic cultures feel inferior and powerless. When a white person calls us a minority then that White person is saying that he is the majority and thus more powerful than you. African Americans should stop parroting the word minority and realize that we are 60-75 million strong in America, something President Barack Obama and his campaign knew and why he was elected to the presidency twice. White people need to understand that we all are neither minority nor majority, just the people of America.

I have often thought that the relationship between Blacks and Whites in America is similar to H. G. Wells' book 'The Time Machine' and the characters, The Eloi and the Morlocks.

America is still a place where Black people have no real power, economic or otherwise and White people know that they have the power to control Black people, by laying siege to the African American Communities with their police, National Guard and Army. White subjugation destroys any dissension, up-rising or anti-American rhetoric that usually begins over the death, plight and suffering of poor ghettoized African Americans.

White America has done this many times over the last two hundred and fifty years. Most people will remember the riots and unsettledness of African American Communities during the Civil Rights Eras of the 1940's, 1950's, 1960's and 1970's and now finally the 2010's.

By the beginning of the 1970's and the 1980's the White government and system had infiltrated our Black communities with heroin and crack in order to pacify, keep down, and destroy any meaningful Black dissension, by addicting millions of African Americans to drugs. Well, it worked, and until the murders of Trayvon Martin, Jordan Davis, Michael Brown, Tamir Rice and to many other unarmed African American children, and the recent protests, a great majority of young people in the ghetto were too busy going to jail, smoking crack, shooting heroin and committing felonies. Too busy to dissent, unify and care about the overwhelming force of a racist white police force killing and jailing our young black men, women and children by the thousands. But, in the 2010's things have changed.

The following plot excerpt from H.G. Wells 'The Time Machine' somewhat describes the African American community of the recent 80's, 90's and 2000's (The Eloi) and the White system that preys and feeds on the Black community and literally takes the food out of our mouths. While at the same time devouring and destroying us and our children devoid of any enlightenment, soul or conscience. (The Morlocks)

H.G. WELLS

In the new narrative, the Time Traveler tests his device with a journey that takes him to A.D. 802,701, where he meets the Eloi, (Black People) a society of small, elegant, childlike adults. They live in small communities within large and futuristic yet slowly deteriorating buildings, doing no work and having a frugivorous diet. His efforts to communicate with them are hampered by their lack of curiosity or discipline, and he speculates that they are a peaceful, common society, the result of humanity conquering nature with technology, and subsequently evolving to adapt to an environment in which strength and intellect are no longer advantageous to survival."

Later in the dark, he is approached menacingly by the Morlocks, (White People) ape-like troglodytes who live in darkness underground and surface only at night. Within their dwellings he discovers the machinery and industry that makes the above-ground paradise possible. He alters his theory, speculating that the human race has evolved into two species: the leisured classes have become the ineffectual Eloi, and the downtrodden working classes have become the brutish light-fearing Morlocks. Deducing that the Morlocks have taken his time machine, he explores the Morlock tunnels, learning that they feed on the Eloi. His revised analysis is that their relationship is not one of lords and servants but of livestock and ranchers. The Time Traveler theorizes that intelligence is the result of and response to danger; with no real challenges facing the Eloi, they have lost the spirit, intelligence, and physical fitness of humanity at its peak. Meanwhile, he saves an Eloi named Weena from drowning as none of the other Eloi take any notice of her plight.

H. G. Wells was an enlightened man who believed fervently in the power of "The White Man" to overcome its basic need to destroy itself through racial purity.

"Wells' 1906 book *The Future in America*, contains a chapter, *The Tragedy of Color*, which discusses the problems facing black Americans. While writing the book, Wells met with Booker T. Washington, who provided him with much of his information for *The Tragedy of Color*. Wells praised the 'heroic' resolve of black Americans, stating *"he doubted if the United States could show any thing finer than the quality of the resolve, the steadfast effort hundreds of Black and colored men are making today to live blamelessly, honorably, and patiently, getting for themselves what scraps of refinement, learning, and beauty they may, keeping their hold on a civilization they are grudged and denied"*.

In this book *The Investigation and Study of the White People of America and Western Europe*, I have kept the words *'white'* and *'black'* instead of who we are, African Americans and European Americans, to describe the people of America so that I can easily define who we are in the everyday language that most Americans use.

It is my hope and dream that one day we can all call one another who we all truly are, 'Americans'.

****

WHAT IS WRONG WITH WHITE PEOPLE

I come from a place that is so invisible that you can hardly see me. Yet, I am despised, hated and feared more than anyone or anything. I am invisible, I live in the real ghetto, the projects. I am poor and hungry, I live in the underbelly of America and I am poor and have nothing. I am a black man, I am a black woman, I am a black child, and I am invisible, until someone kills me or I kill someone.

This book is essentially a children's story. A story of tens of millions of children locked away, in the segregated, red lined ghettos and housing projects of America. Living in a bad and horrific environment, in bad conditions, with bad parents, in bad schools, where death rides hard and is known by everybody.

I found out early on that this was not going to be an easy book to write. I wanted to write an autobiography about my early childhood and teen years and the horrific murderers, pimps, gangsters, drug dealers, drug addicts, rapists, child abusers and thieves, that I grew up with, lived with, called family, and write about in *The Autobiography of an American Ghetto Boy.* I soon realized that I could not write about me as an African American child and teen living in America, without writing about White America, what it was like when I was a child, how it shaped the people around me and what it is like to now live in America, which for tens of millions of African American children is horrific, terrifying, and not so very different than it was for me as a child.

I also wanted to write about what it was like for a child and young teen-ager to grow up in the real ghetto, the projects, and come from a dysfunctional and violent family where contrary to what poor Black people are always depicted as; there was no God, no church on Sunday, no marching with Martin Luther King, Jr., and no singing in the church choir.

I have written this book to show how White racism and White supremacy affected the lives of the people I lived and grew up with. Also as a study of White people and their genetic ability to hate people who are different than them, and I also had wondered if there had ever been a study based on the White People of America.

I also realized that because I was writing an autobiography that I could not and should not leave out the history of my forefathers, my ancestors. That any autobiography from an African American should include my/our forefathers going all the way back to Africa and include the story of what Western Europe and the United States of America did to my African ancestors in Africa and on their journey to America in Slave Ships and include their life in America through Slavery, Cultural Destruction, Emancipation, Reconstruction, Jim Crow, Segregation, Institutional Racism, Inter-Generational Poverty, the Civil Rights Era and the Obama Era.

And because a piece of my heritage and blood is Native American, I thought that I would include a small amount of their journey, and also, because a piece of my heritage and blood is Western European (Portuguese, French and English) I thought that I would include the horrors of that bloodline and the rapes, massacres and enslavement that this bloodline perpetuated on my two other bloodlines, and thus begin '*a study of the White People of America*', who they are and where they come from. My hope is that this will be a beginning into a more complete and complex scientific, college and university level investigation and study of '*The White Man and The White People of America.*'

And I also wrote this book, because, I always hear White American politicians and people always asking this one basic question, '*What is wrong with Black People?*', so because I am a Black people, I thought that I would make an attempt to answer and explain the question '*What is wrong with Black people*'. Well the answer is *White people* and the explanation is inside this book.

Also, because since the day I was born all I have ever heard is White people talking about Black people, maligning Black people, blaming Black people, accusing Black, defining Black people to this very minute, this very second without a clue as to what the fuck they are talking about. And year after year, decade after decade, century after century goes by without White people being defined by Black people. Well, this book defines who White people are, and blames them for everything that has happened to Black people in not only America, but, the world.

The films shot and books written about the Transatlantic Slave Trade Holocaust and Slavery, including **Amistad, Roots** and **Twelve Years a**

Slave, all had White people involved, as either writers, directors, producers or executive producers, and even the writers of the books, Alex Haley, Solomon Northup, etc., all had White people involved as Publishers and Editors. So the true and detailed story of the atrocities and horrors of what the White people of America and Western Europe did to West Africa, Africa, its people for five hundred long years and to the generations of hundreds and hundreds and hundreds of millions of Africans, those of African descent around the world, including African Americans, has never really been told. Who these White people were, what they were, where they came from, what made the White people of Western Europe and America go crazy and have a blood lust and hatred for Africans, Africa, African Americans and people of African descent, to enslave and colonize them for five hundred years has never been told.

It is my hope that the poor, underprivileged, disenfranchised, African Americans in the housing projects and ghettos of urban and rural America and Black Africans throughout West Africa and Africa and the poor People of Color around the world who have been put into generational poverty and cultural destruction through the hypocrisy and greed of the White People of Western Europe and America will by reading this book know that they have nothing to be ashamed of. That the shame is on every White person of Western European and White American background who walks the face of God's green Earth.

And, I wrote this book, because 70% of the White people of America have never, ever, had to or been made to take responsibility or to atone for their sins and the atrocities, horrors and sins of their ancestors. In fact, White people still continue to malign Black people, disrespect Black people, make fun of Black people, pass laws that would hinder and take away Black people's affirmative action and voting rights. All the while, even though the 30% of the White people of America who mean well and try to do everything they can to right the wrong that America has done, still allow their Politicians to continue to blame and make fun of that poor Black mother with three children on food stamps as if she was the cause of all the United States' ills.

Yet America still gives tens and tens of millions of dollars to some tribesmen in Iraq, Syria, and Afghanistan and billions and billions of dollars to other nations and their armies in Egypt, Israel, Pakistan, Iraq, Syria, Afghanistan and Iran, while here in America our military veterans are sleeping in the street and working parents can't make enough to feed their children healthy food and the masses of Black people in America have nothing, but a rat's nest, fucking project or ghetto apartment. These same White politicians and people like Donald Trump have continuously belittled and look down on, lied to, cheat and blame Black people for everything wrong with America, with a smugness that always suggests and says that no atonement, reparation or thought for Black people is necessary for anything, especially the horrors of slavery, Jim Crow and segregation, and that our ancestors' pain, suffering and blood for this country does not and did not matter.

So I thought I would write a book that also tells Black people and especially White people why reparations and atonement from White people and the United States Federal Government is necessary.

And finally I thought, well, everything else has been done to try to repair Race Relations between Blacks and Whites in America; so I thought that I would try to do something different than had ever been done before. Which is to give White people, along with my unique African American childhood and experience, detailed in the *Autobiography of an American Ghetto Boy,* the cold hard facts, *mixed with the truth*, over and over and over and over and over and over, and over, and over, and over again, about what did happen between Black people and White people in Western Europe and America.

After you have read, *An Investigation and Study of the White People of America and Western Europe*, my hope is that White people and Black people will finally understand what happened and why. And that with this knowledge both cultures, both so-called races, will begin a dialogue that can be truly open and honest. Please let me know if I have done that. You can email me at amberbk@aol.com when you have finished reading the book.

By the way, I never went to a College or a University or have gotten a job because of Affirmative Action. In fact, the only person in the United States of America that I personally ever knew, or heard of, who went to a university or got a job because of an Affirmative Action Program, is Supreme Court Justice Clarence Thomas. *I know. You can laugh!*

****

HOW BLACK CHILDREN ARE SEEN BY WHITE AMERICANS

The Trayvon Martins, Jordan Davises, Michael Browns and Tamir Rice's are murdered by 70% of the white people in America. The problem is that the weak white coward is not meeting the real black gangster. The weak white coward is meeting children who watch too much television, listen to too much rap, watch too many rap videos, think that rappers are gangsters, and are emulating as children will do those they consider to be their heroes. As soon as the weak white coward zimmerman said "what are you doing around here" the real black gangster would have shot him dead. As soon as the weak white coward dunn said "turn down that music", the real black gangsters would have shot him dead. As soon as the weak white coward wilson said, "come here", the real black gangster would have shot him dead. None of the weak white cowards would have finished their sentences.

The weak white cowards know this, they know what a real black gangster looks like; they have studied our children and know their language and dress. They know that what they are accosting is a not a real black gangster, the weak white coward is not interested in going up against the real gangster, they know the difference; but, they use the real black gangster as their excuse and defense for killing our children. Trayvon Martin, Jordan Davis, Michael Brown and his friends were not gangsters or thugs, they were seventeen-year-old children.

The weak white coward has bought a gun and carries a gun specifically to kill what they hate, what they are angry about, what they despise, and that is us and our children. The weak white coward also listens to too much rap, watches too many rap videos and thinks that rappers are gangsters; they are not, they are actors, musicians and hustlers; they are not gangsters. The weak white cowards run from the real black gangsters, and never say anything to upset them.

The weak white coward is only interested in the most negative things about our children. The weak white coward is not interested in knowing anything positive about our children, he's not interested in knowing anything about the 98% of our children who are achieving and living good lives. Trayvon Martin, Jordan Davis, Michael Brown and their friends were not gangsters or thugs, they were seventeen-year-old children.

I was raised by real black gangsters. I grew up in a housing project with real black gangsters. I lived with real black gangsters. I knew real black gangsters. At one time, one moment in my life, a long time ago. I was a real black gangster. The people that I lived with, grew up with and write about in my autobiography, *The Autobiography of an American Ghetto Boy,* are real black and white gangsters. These children being killed are not real black gangsters. So if you're not a real black gangster, a real shooter, with blood on your hands, and you are not prepared mentally, physically or emotionally, to blow that weak white coward away and do the time, then just walk away, don't say nothing to that weak white coward; just pray that one day soon the weak white coward makes a bad mistake and has something ignorant to say to the real black gangster.

Just always try to remember that the weak white coward instigates these encounters by talking to our children. If the weak white cowardly "so called men" zimmerman, dunn and wilson had not said anything to these children, the children would be alive.

The gun laws in this country need to be changed, so that the weak white cowards who use guns to burn, lynch and kill us and our children will have to learn to fight with their fists, when they want to open their cowardly mouths and have something untoward to say to us or our children.

AN INVESTIGATION AND STUDY OF
THE WHITE PEOPLE OF AMERICA AND
WESTERN EUROPE

VOLUME ONE

THE INVESTIGATION

CHAPTER 1

I PLEDGE ALLEGIANCE TO THE FLAG

The Poverty, degradation, humiliation, murderers, rapists, drug addicts, drug dealers, child abusers, alcoholics, pimps, prostitutes and the horrendous hunger, that I lived with, grew up with and write about in, *The Autobiography of an American Ghetto Boy*, is all a by-product of Cultural Destruction or as it's called, American Slavery, American Racism, American Segregation, American Jim Crowism and the American Isolationism of millions of poor African Americans into Ghettos and Projects.

The horrific murderers, pimps, gangsters, child abusers, rapists and thieves, along with hard working decent working class Black families that I grew up with, lived with, called family and write about in, *The Autobiography of an American Ghetto Boy,* as do the murderers, pimps, gangsters rapists and thieves who live in our urban African American communities today, are nothing in comparison to the white collar murderers, pimps, gangsters rapists and thieves, posing as politicians, who embody the United States of America Congress, the United States of America Government, The United States of America City and State Governments. They systematically place our Black communities under siege and commit murder, physical and emotional destruction to over tens of millions of poor people in America with the stroke or the non-stroke of a pen every day.

After careful study and research, I have found that 70% of White people in America hate me, dislike me and my culture, wish I didn't exist, want me to go back to Africa, think that I am not human, and if there were not hundreds and hundreds of laws to prevent it, would castrate me, burn me, cut my dick off and lynch me. The other 30% tolerate me, love me and my culture, love my culture, but don't like me, like me, love me and think I could do much better.

While I was writing this book it occurred to me that I could not write the story of my childhood, my youth and the murderers, rapists, drug addicts, child abusers and insane people I grew up with, without writing about the people who made us who we were, without writing about the White people who had shaped our lives and forced us into hunger and poverty, by their laws and greed.

While attending Asa Grey Elementary school we were taught about White history and how brave and wonderful they were, we pledged to the United States of America our allegiance;

I pledge Allegiance to the flag
of the United States of America
and to the Republic for which it stands,
one nation under God, indivisible,
with Liberty and Justice for all.

We were taught how smart White people were, how intelligent and how heroic they were; we were taught that White people were all inclusive, all powerful; we were given their history books, their writers to read, lives to know and be proud of; but us little colored children were not taught why we were segregated against, why we had to live in projects and ghettos. We were not taught that there were thousands of laws in America written for us, most of them against us.

We were not taught why we were hungry, why we had to live on top of each other and why we couldn't live with them. Why we were hated and why we were thought of as nothing or animals in America. Why we were not heroes. Why we had no power. Why we had to live together, all poor, all Black, all hungry, all desperate and without hope. The White teachers were all nice as nice as they could be and I wonder did they know that they weren't teaching us anything about ourselves and who we were. So I thought that I would write about these White people who made us who we are and shaped us and our values in America.

In Western Europe there were hundreds of cultures and sub-cultures, from the English, French, Italian, Dutch, Spanish, German, and Scandinavian. In America all of these cultures became known as White people or the White Race. Their combined one and only real enemy is African Americans.

Every White person no matter where they were from in Western Europe, Eastern Europe, the Scandinavian countries, Canada, South America, Russia, no matter where they came from, once they came to America, they became a White person and the ordained beneficiary of privilege, entitlement and respect. Brought to them exclusively by the murder, massacre, enslavement, rape, killing, segregation and isolation, of Africans, African Americans and Native Americans. They and their White American forefathers are responsible for the murder, massacre, enslavement, rape, killing, segregation, isolation, of African Americans and Native Americans, that legacy gives them their privilege, entitlement and respect, from the United States Government and City, State and County, law enforcement agencies. While Black people are entitled to have no respect from any White man, unless we are entertaining them in sports, music and film.

Black people can never be just regular, average people in America, just working hard for their family. Just walking home with some candy. Just having a bad day. Just playing music a little too loud. Just standing on a corner talking to friends. Just knocking on someone's door to ask for help. Just going for a walk or a run to exercise. Just being an average human being. We always have to be damn near a superhuman athlete or superstar entertainer in order to be respected and survive as a human being and not be told we are up to no good, and subject to suspicion and death from any white person in America.

The Poverty, degradation, humiliation, murder, rape, drug addiction, child abuse, alcoholism, pimps, prostitutes and the horrendous hunger, that I lived with, grew up with and write about in my *Autobiography of an American Ghetto Boy,* is all a product of Cultural Destruction or as you call it American Racism, Jim Crow and Segregation.

CHAPTER 2

SPIT ON WHITE PEOPLE

I do believe that the Universal Creator of the Universe, (GOD) allows some of us, not all of us, to come back to Earth again after we die, and that we get five seconds to remember who we once were, and that Hitler, when he came back as a termite, remembered that he had been Hitler for four seconds before a gorilla ate him, and that the White Transatlantic Slave Ship Captain had three seconds when he came back as a roach to remember all the fun he had raping and killing Africans, before my mother's slipper slapped and squashed him. You don't get to come back twice.

White people are always asking, what's wrong with them, what is wrong with Black people, why can't they get it together, the Jews got it together, the Irish got it together, the Italians got it together, the Polish got it together, we all got it together, what is wrong with those Black people. What's wrong with us?

What's wrong with us Black people is that we didn't come over here on the Mayflower or a fuckin Steamship in 1st, 2nd, or 3rd class steerage.

We came to Europe, to Paris, to France, to London, to Liverpool, to England, to Amsterdam, to the Netherlands, to Madrid, to Spain, to Lisbon, to Portugal, to Berlin, to Germany, to South America, to the Americas, to Jamaica, to Bermuda, to Cuba, to the Virgin Islands, to Aruba, to the Dutch West Indies, to Haiti, to Santa Domingo, to Brazil, to Central America, to the United States, to Antigua, to Anguilla, to Barbuda, to the Bahamas, to Barbados, to Belize, to the British West Indies, to Mexico, to the Cayman Islands, to the United States Virgin Islands, to the Dominican Republic, to Martinique, to Grenada, to Guadeloupe, to Honduras, to Montserrat, to Puerto Rico, to Saint Barthelemy, to Saint Kitts, to Saint Lucia, to Nevis, to the Netherlands, to Antilles, to Saint Martin, to Saint Vincent, to the Grenadines, to Trinidad, to Tobago, to the Turks and Caicos islands, to Pelican Island, to San Andres and Providencia, to Nicaragua, to Venezuela, to Guatemala, to Honduras, to

Costa Rica, to Panama, to Alta Velo, to Brazil, to Guyana, to Colombia, to Venezuela, to Argentina, to St. Helena, to French Guiana, to Bolivia, to Chile, to Ecuador, to Paraguay, to Peru, to Suriname, to Uruguay to the United States of America, not on a fuckin vacation, but on a slave ship, packed in by the thousands, with naked African women and young girls menstruating all over the slave ship, while being raped by White men over and over and over and over and over and over and over and over and over and over and over and over and over and over and over and over again and again and again and again and again and again and again.

Babies being born on slave ships, their heads being bashed against the bull works and then being thrown overboard to the waiting sharks. That's how we came to Western Europe and America.

My Great-Great-Great Grandmother, on my mother's side, was on that ship, along with the tens of millions, hundreds of millions of African men, women, boys and girls who made the trip to Western Europe and the Americas in those slave ships over a four-hundred-year span.

She started her day out in a Sierra Leone village in 1829 as an eleven-year-old girl. She was captured and brought to Bunce Island in Sierra Leone, where she was raped, beaten, sodomized, and made to give blow jobs to many White Englishmen, Dutch and Portuguese traders and sailors. Starved, naked, un-bathed, and forced to live in blood, shit and urine, day and night, only being bathed before she was brought outside the dungeons of the castle to service the many more White men who clamored for her affections. Spoken to in words of love and affection by ghost men in languages she didn't understand.

All of this was before she was chained with thousands of other men and women and boys and girls and brought in terror to the slave ship that would take her to her vacation spot and new home in the Americas, where the white monkeys lived. Where she would be beaten, raped, starved, sodomized, and worked to death in Alabama, Florida, Georgia, Louisiana, Mississippi, South Carolina, Texas, Arkansas, North Carolina, Tennessee, Virginia, Kentucky, Washington, DC, and Maryland.

Forced to watch as her daughters were raped, beaten, and impregnated by white vermin and watch as her sons, her slave husbands, were tortured, beaten, terrorized, sexually abused by White men and women alike and humiliated, lynched, burnt, castrated physically, emotionally, mentally, and spiritually of their manhood. Their manhood taken by vicious, in-human, barbaric and primitive White men, year after year, decade after decade, century after century, to this very day, this very minute, this very second, in relentless poverty and degradation.

Tens of millions, hundreds of millions of African men, women, boys and girls made the trip in these slave ships over a four-hundred-year span. Kept in hundreds of dungeons and castles built and used, up and down the West African coast by the United States of America, Britain, France, Portugal, Spain, Holland, and other Western European nations, to hold and keep these gentle, captured, African farmers and builders, keepers of the land and fishermen of the lakes and oceans, toilers of the land, these gentle African people.

***

The British traders based at Bunce Island shipped hundreds of thousands of African captives to South Carolina, Georgia, Florida, and other South-ern Colonies during the mid- and late 1700s. Rice planters in South Carolina and Georgia were particularly anxious to buy captives from Sierra Leone and other parts of the "Rice Coast" where Africans had grown rice for thousands of years. Slave auction advertisements in 18th century Charles Town (South Carolina) and Savannah (Georgia) often mentioned ships arriving with slaves brought from the "Rice Coast," "Sierra-Leon," and "Bunce Island." African farmers taken from the Rice Coast region made rice one of the most profitable industries in America.

Henry Laurens, a wealthy South Carolina slave dealer and rice planter, was Bunce Island's business agent in Charles Town before the American Revolutionary War. After the war began, Laurens became the President of the Continental Congress, and when the fighting finally ended, he was named one of the American Peace Commissioners who negotiated U.S. Independence under the Treaty of Paris. Amazingly, Richard Oswald, Bunce Island's London-based owner, was appointed head of the British negotiating team in Paris. In other words, United States Independence was negotiated, in part, between Bunce Island's British owner and his American business agent in South Carolina. The relationship between these two men reflects Bunce Island's importance in the commerce that linked Britain, North America, and West Africa during the Colonial Pe-riod.

23

Bunce Island was also linked to the Northern Colonies. Slave ships from Rhode Island, Massachusetts, Connecticut; and New York frequently called at the castle, taking their human cargoes to the West Indies or back to the Southern Colonies. These Northern slave ships often purchased their African captives with rum produced in New England with molasses brought back to North America from the West Indies.

***

AFRICA'S SLAVE CASTLES

The last place an African would 'reside' before going through the "door-of-no-return" to slavery in the Americas.

It is virtually impossible to write about the Slave Castles without describing the brutality of the African slave trade, the most evil and insidious holocaust of human beings in history, which was perpetrated primarily by White Europeans on the Black African (men, women and children).

It was not only the physical being that was captured and destroyed, it was the mind, soul and spirit of millions of Black people who were uprooted and transplanted. According to research, what is referred to as the African slave trade began around the latter half of the 15th century when Europeans captured and sold Blacks to White traders as porters.

Looking at a map of Africa at the beginning of the 20th century--when slavery was supposedly abolished--it can be described as the United States of Europe. These human traffickers may have proclaimed the end of slavery but colonialism and imperialism lingered on in Africa as a way of life for Blacks. The continent was divided up among the Belgians, the British, the Dutch, the French, the Germans, the Italians, the Portuguese and the Spanish and in many ways controlled by the United States of America.

The European slave traffickers had castles built along the West Coast of Africa close to the sea to facilitate easy access of their human cargo onto ships. The conditions of the castles reflected their attitudes and treatment of Black slaves. To be able to eliminate vacancies, and to ensure a constant supply of slaves, the Europeans instigated conflicts between the tribes which led to continuous wars. The ensuing wars produced able-bodied men, children-bearing women and even children who were yoked together and held for weeks in the dungeons of the slave castles until ships arrived, ships that took the slaves to Europe, North and South America, and the Caribbean.

Life in the castles for the slaves was a living hell on earth before the perilous voyage across the ocean in the hole of a ship. At the beginning, the need for the slave trade appeared to be basic economics; Whites needed lots of free labor to work their colonial possessions and they surmised Blacks would fill that labor void. The stay in the dungeon lasted about four to six weeks and it was not subliminal; it was real and it was physical. The men and the women were separated. Some of the women were used as servants in the castle. Conditions in the castle were wretched; the slaves were packed in, literally like sardines in a can. One of the purposes of the stay was to break the spirit of the men so by the time the ships arrived, they would be docile and ready for what was next. It was an unknown prelude of what was to come on the ship on the other side of the infamous door-of-no-return. That doorway was aptly named.

Europeans who came to the Gold Coast built castles and forts (fortified trading posts), and they engaged in serious competition among themselves over the natural resources of the continent. But that competition paled in comparison to the bitter rivalry they engineered among the tribal chiefs. They employed the divide-and-conquer mechanism to the maximum. What started as a trade commerce between Africans and Western Europeans evolved into the slave trade.

****

Gold was one of the most precious metals sought after in those days as the only reliable means of conducting international trade--it was common in all countries. The Gold Coast was named for the reservoir of gold it contained. It seemed natural that the combination of gold and slaves would create the ideal place for the Europeans to "set up shop" and build permanent lodgings: castles for "Black" gold and natural gold. Gold Coast was located more strategically than any other African coastal area. Referred to as the "Land of the Blacks," word went to European monarchs of the fertile and populous land rich in gold, ivory and other natural resources, and they sent their explorers out to search for this land. The trading started off as commercial ventures dealing mostly in gold and ivory. Then it attracted so many different European nations that the castles (and forts) became a necessary form of survival and protection, just as they had been in Europe. In addition, it gave the marauders front row access to a profitable market and easy access to the sea.

During the period of active, trans-oceanic slave-trading, hundreds of slave castles were built along the coast of West Africa--from Senegal to Ghana (formerly Gold Coast) however, slaves that were brought, bought and housed therein were also from the interior of the continent. In addition to Cape Coast Castle, other castles and forts included Elmina Castle, Osu Castle aka Fort Christiansborg, Bunce Island and Goree Island. Sometimes villages and towns would arise around the castles and forts which were considered the focal point of the settlement--the civic center. The plan called for traders to purchase, capture or barter for the slaves, imprison them in the castles and finally transfer them to waiting ships as the ships arrive to begin the slaves' last ride along the infamous Middle Passage. The castles were dubbed "warehouses of Black humanity."

The Cape Coast Castle was built initially for commercial trading between Africans and Europeans. (It was similar to the American Indians "greeting" the Pilgrims on the other side of the world). It was first built in timber and later rebuilt in stone. Its ownership changed many times as the Europeans battled for dominancy of the region. At various times, it was occupied by the Dutch, the Swedes and the British (1664), who used it as the seat of their colonial administration. (It is important to note that though the British boasted about abolishing the slave trade, they kept a colonial grip on countries throughout the world infusing them, including parts of Africa, with their white superiority agenda. So too, did their European brethren.) Not until 1957 did Ghana achieve its independence.

In the dungeons, there were hundreds and perhaps thousands of slaves housed at the same time awaiting transportation; there were no toilet facilities. Slaves ate and slept in the same place; they urinated and relieved themselves in the same place. A channel in the floor would carry the waste away from one point to another along the floor. Taking baths was out of the question and there was barely enough ventilation to keep them alive.

***

Elmina Castle was established prior to the Cape Coast Castle centered around an African fishing village port. Before the slave trade thrived, the village was a hub of commercial and social activity centering around a fort that had been built by the Portuguese. As the need for slaves was becoming more apparent, the castle was built in anticipation of the pending mass trafficking of the Black cargo. Even though the Portuguese may have been the ones who entered the slave enterprise on a mass scale, the British took it to a whole new level. They (the British) became innovators of the business and made it into a highly specialized industry; they made it white and "respectable."

The operation of Elmina Castle was used as the model from which many of the other castles took their lead. Those castles were the last place tens of millions of Africans would see of their homeland. The slave trade continued for over four centuries and at the peak of the trafficking, the average castle would account for approximately 150,000 bodies per year. And to fully understand the scope of this human atrocity, life in the slave castle was a mild microcosm of the slaves' future--the journey across the oceans was the beginning of eternal horror and slavery, for those who survived the voyage.

In order to keep the castles' dungeons filled with a consistent flow of Black African bodies, Europeans employed many devious means including goods for slaves, the basis of the triangular trade. Finished goods and other imports were brought to the Coast of West Africa, on the first leg of the triangle. On the second leg, slaves, usually housed in the castle dungeons, were transported to Europe, the Americas and the Caribbean to be sold. The ships then returned to Europe filled with monetary rewards to be filled up again as the third leg of the triangle.

One of the way-stations along the route was Goree Island, one of the first places in Africa that was settled by the Europeans. The island was more significant as a memorial to the slave trade than the activities that transpired there. It was said to have been more of a transient port-of-call than a permanent location. However, the trading of slaves did go on there and from that perspective, it could be considered in terms of guilt by association. (In modern times, Goree Island has been visited by many prominent westerners to dramatize the horrors of the slave trade across the Atlantic.

Though it was not as well-known, Bunce Island was the site of one of the largest slave castles on the West African Coast, located in Sierra Leone. Its location was considered vitally and strategically important as a shipping port for slaves; it was West Africa's largest harbor, which made it important for shipping purposes. The modern computer, through enhanced technology, has been able to produce life-like renditions of images of Bunce Island as it was during the days of slave trading.

As was previously stated, though the Europeans and the United States proclaimed the abolition of slavery and by inference, the castles became residential rather than commercial, the Europeans still occupied most of Africa and brutally enforced their will on Black Africans. This was evidenced by the Berlin West African Conference of 1884-1885 where the Europeans laid claim to virtually all of Africa. Parts of the continent had been "explored," but now representatives of European governments and rulers went into the continent to create and/or expand strangleholds of influence for Europe. This conference laid the groundwork for the now familiar politico-geographical/physical occupation of Africa, and many of the slave castles became civic centers from where they administrated their ill-gotten colonial possessions.

Unlike many other horrible human tragedies, there was no photography during the slave trade therefore, much of what has been reported came through stories passed down, drawings and scrolls that were left, archaeological diggings, advancement in technology and most importantly through the souls of Black folks.

CHAPTER 3

STARVING, STINKING AND RAPED

It would seem, that one hundred and fifty-two years after Abraham Lincoln Emancipated the Confederated Southern States Slaves, 99% who because of the strict southern laws against educating slaves, could not read, write or do math, held no land, did not know where they were, had no money, did not have any understanding of the American or European financial system, had no real understanding of the power of money, and held no power over their lives whatsoever. And so with all that against them, you would still think that 150 years after the civil war, that the great majority of African Americans should have been assimilated into the American dream of economic middle class wealth and prosperity.

But, imagine ten million slaves freed and out on the road in the American South for the first time, but not really free, all different skin colors, because of the sexual ferociousness of the plantation slave master, slave farmers and White men in general for African and Black women. There were hundreds of thousands, millions of just about white slaves, high yella light skinned slaves, light and bright skinned slaves, light brown skinned slaves, brown skinned slaves, slaves of all different colors mixed with the millions of White men who had raped and impregnated the mothers, grandmothers, great grandmothers, great-great-great-great-great-great-great grandmothers of these slaves for over two hundred years in America.

And then imagine, ten million freed slaves. Hated by just about every White person in America, especially in the south. Hated and beaten, maligned, despised, used, abused, spit on, made fun of, talked about, no money, no clothes, no horse, no buggy, no housing, no lodging, homeless, lynched, burned, starving, stinking, unwashed, disrespected, no jobs, no work, no money, segregated against, terrorized, no citizenship, shot, killed, hunted, raped, sodomized, arrested, blamed for theft, and a million things like rapes that they didn't do, then lynched.

Hated by every White man you see, because they can't get over what they had done to us and it made them hate us even more for being in existence, taking up space, trying to take jobs away from decent White folks, breathing the very air that White people breathe, they kept them out, segregated against them. White men passed laws against the Coloreds very existence, until they went back into slavery as sharecroppers with no economic security whatsoever, and no financial knowledge of the White American financial system at all.

My Great-Great-Great Grandmother would have been on that same road, where some slaves went west to find their manhood working on the railroads or becoming what would be called Buffalo Soldiers for the United States Army and others went north on what would be the first mass migration of African Americans in America.

My Great-Great-Great Grandmother who was now forty-seven years old, black skinned as Africa, had birthed eight children, some for her slave masters and some from her husbands, five who had been sold. She went north, walking from the cotton fields of Georgia, with her three all different colored, remaining children, one of whom was my Great-Great Grandmother born in slavery in Georgia and having her second child, my Great Grandmother born in Virginia in 1866.

A freeborn girl named Daisy, who I would know in the fifties as a skittish, tall, skinny old woman, who talked in a high pitched voice and who along with her husband named Daddy Herbert, and her assorted sisters and aunts, had come down through the ages, through Virginia, Baltimore, Maryland, to Boston, Massachusetts along with my Grandmother and her two sisters and one brother, where they would face like millions of other African Americans, thousands of laws passed legally and illegally across the south and north that would stop them from attaining decent jobs, a decent education, decent housing and restricted to a life of poverty inside a city or rural ghetto, where they and their men, for the least offense, could be lynched, burnt, castrated and their limbs pulled apart for the enjoyment of White people.

***

There are a tens of tens of millions of White people in America today, whose grandparents, great grandparents, great-great grandparents, great-great-great grandparents had picnics, barbeques, and social gatherings while watching Black men being lynched, burnt alive, castrated and pulled apart, and Black women, disfigured, lynched, burnt alive, and shot numerous times as sport for White men.

The movies *Birth of A Nation* and *Gone With the Wind*, became the foundation of what White people thought Black people were like and has rippled down White family through White family for over a hundred years.

Every White family in America from Montana to Arizona, from Wyoming to California to Florida. From Massachusetts to Georgia, from Alabama to Illinois, from Mississippi to New York, every White family, every White person, in every state and city and town and village in America saw *The Birth of a Nation*. A 1915 American silent drama film directed by D. W. Griffith and based on the novel and play *The Clansman,* both by Thomas Dixon, Jr.

D. W. Griffith co-wrote the screenplay with Frank E. Woods, and co-produced the film with Harry Aitken. It was released on February 8, 1915. The film was originally presented in two parts, separated by an intermission. It was the first 12-reel film in America. The film chronicles the relationship of two families in Civil War and Reconstruction-US era: the pro-Union Northern Stonemans and the pro-Confederacy Southern Cameroons over the course of several years. The assassination of President Abraham Lincoln by John Wilkes Booth is dramatized.

The film was a commercial success, but was highly controversial owing to its portrayal of Black men played by White actors in blackface as unintelligent and sexually aggressive towards White women, and the portrayal of the Ku Klux Klan whose original founding is dramatized as a heroic force.

There were nationwide African-American protests against *The Birth of a Nation,* including in Boston. The NAACP spearheaded an unsuccessful campaign to ban the film, while thousands of White Bostonians and millions of White people across the nation flocked to see it. The film is also credited as one of the events that inspired the formation of the "second era" Ku Klux Klan at Stone Mountain, Georgia, in the same year. *The Birth of a Nation* was used as a recruiting tool for the KKK. Under the segregationist Ku Klux Klansman Democratic Party President of the United States of America, President Woodrow Wilson, it became the first motion picture to be screened in the White House.

Despite the film's controversial content, Griffith's innovative film techniques make it one of the most influential films in the commercial film industry, and it is often ranked as one of the greatest American films of all time and every White person in America saw it.

With *Gone With The Wind* every white family in America from Montana to Arizona, from Wyoming to California to Florida, from Massachusetts to Georgia, from Alabama to Illinois, from Mississippi to New York, every white family, every white person, in every state and city and town and village in America saw *Gone With The Wind* a 1939 American epic historical romance film adapted from Margaret Mitchell's Pulitzer-winning 1936 novel.

It was produced by David O. Selznick of Selznick International Pictures, directed by Victor Fleming and starred Clark Gable, Vivian Leigh and Hattie McDaniel. Both films have shaped the thoughts of every White American and every White American family towards Black Americans and how White Americans think Black people act, talk, think, what we think about, who we are, and how White Americans related to Black Americans in a very negative way for three generations.

Only the advent of MTV and possibly the Bill Cosby show, both created in the early 1980's, began to change the thinking of how a new younger generation of White children and teenagers began to see Black people in a more positive light, as human beings, as more Black people began to show up on National Television. *Well, that is until Gangster Rap took over.*

CHAPTER 4

WHITE OPPRESION AND TERRORISM

The Transatlantic Slave Trade was just during the first 100 years from 1500-1600, bathed in a horror, brutality and violence so vast that the human mind cannot really comprehend or understand that One Hundred Million human beings were killed, abused and raped in ways so horrific that in this world, and I know this will be hard for you to believe, that the nice people that you see in Spain, Portugal, England, Holland, Belgium, France, and other Western European countries are the direct descendants of the monsters who raped, destroyed, killed and enslaved millions of African people, a year, in just West Africa alone.

The funny thing is that although tens of millions of White Western European and after 1776 White American men, women, corporations, institutions, insurance companies, etc., participated in the Atlantic Slave Trade and Slavery in Western Europe and the United States of America, that just like Nazi Germany after World War Two, you cannot find one white person who will stand up and say, yes, in my family, in my family tree, in my corporation, there were people who were slave ship captains and sailors, in my family tree there are men who participated in the horrors of African Chattel Slavery in the United States of America, South America, the Caribbean and Western Europe.

As in Nazi Germany where every German citizen benefited from the extermination and destruction of Jews until Nazi Germany was destroyed. So has every White person in America, to this very day, benefited from the pain, suffering and slave labor of my Great-Great-Great Grandmother and my Great-Great-Great-Great-Great-Great-Great Grandparents on both sides of my family and their children's, children's, children's, children's, children's, children's, children's, children's, children's, children. To this very day, to this very minute, to this very second, the pain, suffering and blood of my Great-Great-Great Grandmother still exists today in the housing projects, in the ghettos, in the people that I write about in this book.

It exists in the tens of millions of inter-generational poor black people in America today, right now, and there is nothing the United States of

America can do about it, except apologize for the horrors of slavery and pay reparations in the form of free economic, business and financial courses for every African American, born from the blood of slaves, 17-25 years old, at the college or university of their choice. And that would include Harvard and Stanford Universities. Because in America although my ancestors were freed from slavery and began their long walk to freedom, almost one hundred and fifty years ago, we are not yet freed from social and economic oppression.

White people always point to President Barack Obama as a "see how much you have attained"; you should be satisfied. But President Barack Obama is not from the blood of slaves. His mother was a White woman and his father a pure bred African from Kenya with not one drop of White blood in him. I'll only be satisfied when there have been, two, then three, then four and then maybe five, African American Presidents of the United States of America, all from the blood of American Slaves.

But, what makes President Barack Obama a great man and one of the greatest Presidents of the United States of America is that he was born into a country that gives no privilege, that gives nothing to people born non-white and yet he a non-white became the leader of that nation and fought for those who have no rights or privileges. He fought alone, without backup, knowing that the people he fights for, the poor, the weak, the hungry, the medically uninsured, the underprivileged Black, White, Asian, Native American, and Gay people, with no real power, could not protect him from those who wished to destroy him and his policies. Yet he fought every day, every second of his presidency for them, for us.

As I said in my book, 'African American History in the United States of America—An Anthology—From Africa to President Barack Obama, Volume One', *"Because of the past horrors of American History, those four African American people, living in the White House at 1600 Pennsylvania Avenue, Washington, DC; President Barack Obama, The First Lady Michelle Obama and their children, Malia Ann Obama and Natasha Obama are the four bravest people to ever live there and the four bravest people in the United States of America."*

CHAPTER 5

WHITE MEN, SEX, AND SLAVES

The fact is whole countries and a new culture of people arose from the millions of African and African American woman raped each year for five hundred years and more, and forced to bear the children of these White savages and a new human being of lighter color and texture called a **Mulatto**—The term **mulatto** was used to designate a person who was biracial, with one black parent and one white parent.

A **Quadroon**—Quadroon was used to designate a person of one-quarter African ancestry that is one biracial parent (African descent and white) and one white parent; in other words, one African grandparent and three white grandparents.

In South America, which had a variety of terms for racial groups, some terms for quadroons were **Morisco** or **Chino**.

The term **Octoroon** referred to a person with one-eighth African/Aboriginal ancestry; that is, someone with family heritage of one biracial grandparent; in other words, one African great-grandparent and seven European great-grandparents. As with the use of *quadroon*, this word was applied to a limited extent in Australia for those of one-eighth Aboriginal ancestry, as the government implemented assimilation policies. In Latin America, a term for octoroon is *albino*.

Terceron—**Terceron** was a term synonymous with **octoroon,** derived from being three generations of descent from an African ancestor (great-grandparent).

The term **Mustee** was also used to refer to a person with one-eighth African ancestry, while **mustefino** refers to a person with one-sixteenth African ancestry. The terms **Quintroon** or **Hexadecaroon**" were also used.

In some cases, it became a general term to refer to all persons of mixed race. In Latin America, the terms **Griffe** or **Sambo** were sometimes used for an individual of three-quarters African heritage, or the child of a biracial parent and a fully Black parent.

In the American South, before, during and after the antebellum period, African and African American slaves, male and female, were used as sex slaves by White women and White men. Sometimes whole plantations and sections of the South swarmed with the interbreeding of just about white, almost white and light skinned children of these so-called sexually taboo relationships that never seemed to be against the law for white men. On the contrary, a white woman caught fucking a Black slave could and was often killed along with the slave, usually by her husband or neighbors.

She was usually whipped first and then made to watch as her Black lover was burnt alive, while his dick was cut off. She was then usually hanged, and more than not, with his Black dick hanging from her mouth.

During the antebellum period, abolitionists featured thousands of mulattoes and other light-skinned former slaves in public forums and lectures in the North, to arouse public sentiments against slavery by showing Northerners the hypocrisy and sexual degradation the Southern White Male was capable of doing during slavery.

85% of every light skinned or brown colored African American person in America is the direct result of millions of American White men brutally raping African American Women slaves from 1650-1865. That would include the first and second Presidents of the United States of America, George Washington, Thomas Jefferson and many other American Presidents after them.

Presidents of the United States of America who owned slaves: President George Washington; President Thomas Jefferson; President James Madison; President James Monroe; President Andrew Jackson; President Martin Van Buren; President William Henry Harrison; President John Tyler; President James Polk; President Zachary Taylor; President Andrew Johnson; President Ulysses S. Grant.

Known Presidents of the United States of America who raped Black women who were slaves: President George Washington; President Thomas Jefferson; President Andrew Jackson; President William Henry Harrison; President John Tyler; President James Polk; President Zachary Taylor.

Known Presidents of the United States of America who raped and fucked Black women who were slaves and had children by some of the Black women they raped: President George Washington; President Thomas Jefferson; President Andrew Jackson; President John Tyler.

Presidents of the United States of America who tried to do something and better the plight of Slaves and African Americans in the United States in order of importance: President Barack Obama; President Abraham Lincoln; President Lyndon Baines Johnson; President Richard Nixon; President John F. Kennedy; President Franklin Delano Roosevelt; President Bill Clinton; President Teddy Roosevelt; President George W. Bush; President George H. W. Bush; President Harry Truman; President Jimmy Carter; President John Adams, President John Quincy Adams; President Dwight D. Eisenhower.

Presidents of the United States of America who were slave holders, racists, segregationist, Ku Klux Klan members or former Ku Klux Klan members, include President Woodrow Wilson who was all of the above and included all but some of those named in the immediate above, and that would include Johnson and Nixon who in some ways repented of their segregationist ways and helped pass laws that helped the plight of African Americans.

Most of the Founding Fathers of the United States of America were slaveholders and slave traders. They fucked as many Black slave woman as they could. Their first sex when they were fifteen or sixteen was by raping a Black slave girl. Their light-skinned children were usually sold for huge profits for them and their families. And they explored the deepest recesses of inter-breeding and medical experimentations with their slaves to make lighter and more profitable house slaves for the Deep South.

When a White man or White woman had sex with an American Black slave woman or man during the Two Hundred and Fifty years of slavery in the United States it was rape, because that Black slave had no power over anything a White man or White woman did to them.

****

THE WILLIE LYNCH LETTER

This speech was said to have been delivered by Willie Lynch on the bank of the James River in the colony of Virginia in 1712. Lynch was a British slave owner in the West Indies. He was invited to the colony of Virginia in 1712 to teach his methods to slave owners there.

Greetings,

Gentlemen. I greet you here on the bank of the James River in the year of our Lord one thousand seven hundred and twelve. First, I shall thank you, the gentlemen of the Colony of Virginia, for bringing me here. I am here to help you solve some of your problems with slaves. Your invitation reached me on my modest plantation in the West Indies, where I have experimented with some of the newest, and still the oldest, methods for control of slaves. Ancient Rome would envy us if my program is implemented.

As our boat sailed south on the James River, named for our illustrious King, whose version of the Bible we cherish, I saw enough to know that your problem is not unique. While Rome used cords of wood as crosses for standing human bodies along its highways in great numbers, you are here using the tree and the rope. I caught the whiff of a dead slave hanging from a tree, a couple miles back. You are not only losing valuable stock by hangings, you are having uprisings, slaves are running away, your crops are sometimes left in the fields too long for maximum profit, you suffer occasional fires, your animals are killed. Gentlemen, you know what your problems are; I do not need to elaborate. I am not here to enumerate your problems; I am here to introduce you to a method of solving them.

In my bag here, I HAVE A FOOL PROOF METHOD FOR CONTROLLING YOUR BLACK SLAVES. I guarantee every one of you that, if installed correctly, IT WILL CONTROL THE SLAVES FOR AT LEAST (300) THREE HUNDRED YEARS. My method is simple. Any member of your family or your overseer can use it. I HAVE OUTLINED A NUMBER OF DIFFERENCES AMONG THE SLAVES; AND I

40

TAKE THESE DIFFERENCES AND MAKE THEM BIGGER. I USE FEAR, DISTRUST AND ENVY FOR CONTROL PURPOSES.

These methods have worked on my modest plantation in the West Indies and it will work throughout the South. Take this simple little list of differences and think about them. On top of my list is *"AGE,"* but it's there only because it starts with an "a." The second is *"COLOR"* or shade. There is INTELLIGENCE, SIZE, SEX, SIZES OF PLANTATIONS, STATUS on plantations, ATTITUDE of owners, whether the slaves live in the valley, on a hill, East, West, North, South, have fine hair, course hair, or is tall or short.

Now that you have a list of differences, I shall give you an outline of action, but before that, I shall assure you that DISTRUST IS STRONGER THAN TRUST AND ENVY STRONGER THAN ADULATION, RESPECT OR ADMIRATION. The Black slaves after receiving this indoctrination shall carry on and will become self-refueling and self-generating for HUNDREDS of years, maybe THOUSANDS.

Don't forget, you must pitch the **OLD** black male vs. the **YOUNG** black male, and the **YOUNG** black male against the **OLD** black male. You must use the **DARK** skin slaves vs. the **LIGHT** skin slaves, and the **LIGHT** skin slaves vs. the **DARK** skin slaves. You must use the **FEMALE** vs. the **MALE**, and the **MALE** vs. the **FEMALE**.

You must also have white overseers [who] distrust all Blacks. But it is NECESSARY THAT YOUR SLAVES TRUST AND DEPEND ON US. THEY MUST LOVE, RESPECT AND TRUST ONLY US. Gentlemen, these kits are your keys to control. Use them. Have your wives and children use them, never miss an opportunity. IF USED INTENSELY FOR ONE YEAR, THE SLAVES THEMSELVES WILL REMAIN PERPETUALLY DISTRUSTFUL. Thank you gentlemen."

****

LET'S MAKE A SLAVE

It was the interest and business of slave holders to study human nature, and the slave nature in particular, with a view to practical results. I and many of them attained astonishing proficiency in this direction. They had to deal not with earth, wood and stone, but with men and, by every regard, they had for their own safety and prosperity they needed to know the material on which they were to work, conscious of the injustice and wrong they were every hour perpetuating and knowing what they themselves would do. Were they the victims of such wrongs? They were constantly looking for the first signs of the dreaded retribution. They watched therefore with skilled and practiced eyes, and learned to read with great accuracy, the state of mind and heart of the slave, through his sable face. Unusual sobriety, apparent abstractions, sullenness and indifference indeed, any mood out of the common was afforded ground for suspicion and inquiry.

Frederick Douglas LET'S MAKE A SLAVE is a study of the scientific process of man-breaking and slave-making. It describes the rationale and results of the '*Anglo Saxons'* ideas and methods of insuring the master/slave relationship. LET'S MAKE A SLAVE "The Original and Development of a Social Being Called 'The Negro.'"

Let us make a slave. What do we need? First of all, we need a black nigger man, a pregnant nigger woman and her baby nigger boy. Second, we will use the same basic principle that we use in breaking a horse, combined with some more sustaining factors. What we do with horses is that we break them from one form of life to another; that is, we reduce them from their natural state in nature. Whereas nature provides them with the natural capacity to take care of their offspring, we break that natural string of independence from them and thereby create a dependency status, so that we may be able to get from them useful production for our business and pleasure.

CARDINAL PRINCIPLES FOR MAKING A NEGRO

For fear that our future generations may not understand the principles of breaking both of the beasts together, the nigger and the horse. We understand that short range planning economics results in periodic economic chaos; so that to avoid turmoil in the economy, it requires us to have breadth and depth in long range comprehensive planning, articulating both skill and sharp perceptions.

We lay down the following principles for long range comprehensive economic planning. Both horse and niggers are no good to the economy in the wild or natural state. Both must be BROKEN and TIED together for orderly production. For orderly future, special and particular attention must be paid to the FEMALE and the YOUNGEST offspring. Both must be CROSSBRED to produce a variety and division of labor. Both must be taught to respond to a peculiar new LANGUAGE. Psychological and physical instruction of CONTAINMENT must be created for both.

We hold the six cardinal principles as truth to be self-evident, based upon following the discourse concerning the economics of breaking and tying the horse and the nigger together, all inclusive of the six principles laid down above. NOTE: Neither principle alone will suffice for good economics. All principles must be employed for orderly good of the nation. Accordingly, both a wild horse and a wild or natural nigger is dangerous even if captured, for they will have the tendency to seek their customary freedom and, in doing so, might kill you in your sleep. You cannot rest. They sleep while you are awake, and are awake while you are asleep.

They are DANGEROUS near the family house and it requires too much labor to watch them away from the house. Above all, you cannot get them to work in this natural state. Hence, both the horse and the nigger must be broken; that is breaking them from one form of mental life to another. KEEP THE BODY, TAKE THE MIND! In other words, break the will to resist. Now the breaking process is the same for both the horse and the nigger, only slightly varying in degrees. But, as we said before, there is an art in long range economic planning.

YOU MUST KEEP YOUR EYE AND THOUGHTS ON THE FE-MALE **and the** OFFSPRING of the horse and the nigger. A brief discourse in offspring development will shed light on the key to sound economic principles. Pay little attention to the generation of original breaking, but CONCENTRATE ON FUTURE GENERATION. Therefore, if you break the FEMALE mother, she will BREAK the offspring in its early years of development; and when the offspring is old enough to work, she will deliver it up to you, for her normal female protective tendencies will have been lost in the original breaking process.

For example, take the case of the wild stud horse, a female horse and an already infant horse and compare the breaking process with two captured nigger males in their natural state, a pregnant nigger woman with her infant offspring. Take the stud horse, break him for limited containment. Completely break the female horse until she becomes very gentle, whereas you or anybody can ride her in her comfort. Breed the mare and the stud until you have the desired offspring. Then, you can turn the stud to freedom until you need him again. Train the female horse whereby she will eat out of your hand, and she will in turn train the infant horse to eat out of your hand, also.

When it comes to breaking the uncivilized nigger, use the same process, but vary the degree and step up the pressure, so as to do a complete reversal of the mind. Take the meanest and most restless nigger, strip him of his clothes in front of the remaining male niggers, the female, and the nigger infant, tar and feather him, tie each leg to a different horse faced in opposite directions, set him afire and beat both horses to pull him apart in front of the remaining niggers.

The next step is to take a bullwhip and beat the remaining nigger males to the point of death, in front of the female and the infant.

Don't kill him, but PUT THE FEAR OF GOD IN HIM, for he can be useful for future breeding.

CHAPTER 6

SUB HUMANS OR SUPER HUMANS

70% of the White people of the United States of America have on their family trees, people who bought, sold, traded, raped, beat, lynched, castrated, burned, worked to death, segregated against, chained, murdered, jailed, burnt their homes down and terrorized Black people and massacred Native Americans. The police and people who hate Black people, they didn't just wake up one morning and say *I hate Black people*. It is in their blood and goes way back. Most of the 70% of White people who hate Black people, hate Black people because their families always hated Black people, because they hate themselves.

You would think that those people and their politicians would have enough to talk about with the millions of poor and uneducated White people in this country on welfare and food stamps. I feel bad about all those poor White people who don't have no one to speak up for them, because their politicians and city governments are so worried about us kneegrows. At least President Barack Obama looked out for those poor White people with the Affordable Health Care Act.

During the two hundred and fifteen years of slavery in the America the best builders, masonries, bricklayers, carpenters, agriculturists, farmers, workers in America, Europe, South America, the Caribbean, in the world, were African and African American Slaves. After slavery ended in the United States of America 98% of the slaves went to work as sharecroppers, all the while being terrorized by the Whites all around them. The cruel and inhuman treatment of Black people went on all through what is called the Jim Crow era. So that tens of thousands of Black men and woman were destroyed mentally or killed by Whites in America every year, right up through the Civil Rights era, right up until today.

****

The main way the White system has for systematically destroying Black men and Black families is to withhold skilled jobs. The White system kept Black men from holding jobs in unions where after two generations African Americans went from being the best builders, masonries, bricklayers, carpenters, agriculturists, farmers, workers in America to not being able to get union jobs or any jobs, because these jobs went to White men. And right up until now, regular, average Black men cannot get good paying jobs in America.

As long as 70% of White Americans keeps denying what they, their forefathers and America have done to Black Americans under the shame of chattel slavery, segregation, degradation, white supremacy and isolationism; creating impoverished and isolated communities in America that lack the proper educational and nutritional facilities that privileged White communities have; then the people that I lived with, grew up with and wrote about in, *The Autobiography of an American Ghetto Boy,* people who existed in the 1950's and 1960's, will keep existing today and tomorrow just as they existed two hundred years ago; broken, mentally deficient, degraded, unable to know who they are, where they are and where they are going, and will exist the same way one hundred years from now.

Keep denying that White America bought, sold and raped our women and children, tore our families apart, and created generational and institutional poverty. Keep denying that the White American system is based on uneducated black and white people at each other's throats and America will never change and the people that I write about Black and White will keep existing in America forever.

When I was a child we used to call White people "Ugly White Ghosts", because that's what they looked like to us. After a long while and as I got older, I began to see that they thought of themselves as beautiful and perfect, and not only that, I found out later that because their skin was white, they actually thought that they were better and smarter than anyone else on the planet Earth. They thought and still think, that no other person or culture was or is as beautiful or intelligent as they are.

What they didn't tell anybody was that they were killers, who would kill anyone for the most depraved and unscrupulous reasons. Which somehow always ends up being world domination and greed. Oh, and let us not forget it was all for their children. Well, after many years of study and research, I found that they were neither beautiful nor were they perfect. In fact, most of the world's ills were and are caused through their mistakes, lies and deceits. I found that these people were born killers, who hated themselves, as much as they had hated the nobles in Western Europe who enslaved them as serfs and peasants, and were genetically programmed to hate anyone who did not look like them, act like them or worship like them and that would include each other.

****

70% of all White Americans are racists. They hate, fear, and dislike Black people and our culture. They think Black people are animals and fear Black Men's dicks. They think and talk about Black people all the time. When you work with them on the job, they always find a way to make you feel uncomfortable. They make you hate going to work and want to quit your job.

30% of White Americans are okay.... not racists. They love, like and get along with Black people and our culture. They think black people are human beings and don't fear and hate Black men's dicks. They don't think or talk about Black people all the time. When you work with them on the job, they have fun, are comfortable with themselves, and you love going to work, and don't want to quit your job.

70% of White Americans want Black Americans to think that they are smarter, obey all the laws, all the time, obey traffic regulations, are more intelligent, are not lazy, more powerful, don't do drugs, don't sell drugs, live better, are not poor, are not on welfare, do not use food stamps, do no crime, do not commit adultery, do not cheat on their wives and husbands, do not lie, do not steal, do not do cocaine, do not smoke marijuana, do not go to jail, do not rob people, do not shoplift, are not on welfare, are not uneducated, do not smoke crack, do not run red lights, do not drive with their brake lights out, do not drive drunk, do not cheat on their taxes, do not commit murder, do not cuss and swear, do not have and want sex with Black people, especially Black prostitutes, do not cheat on their wives, do not beat their wives and girlfriends and sexually and physically abuse their children.

White Americans believe that there will be a race war in the United States of America, which is why they are teaching their children how to use sub-machine guns and stockpiling millions of guns and other war weapons. White Americans have no patience for Black, Brown or Red People, they think they are smarter, faster, and more hardworking then people of color. White Americans do not read books by Black people, they do not know or care about Black culture or history, all they know is that Black people were once slaves and Martin Luther King, Jr. saved them. 70% of White Americans do not know anything or care anything about Black history or culture, Hispanic History or culture, Native American History or culture, Asiatic History or culture.

But all Black Americans know that 70% of all White people are liars, thieves, steal, murder, kill, do drugs, smoke drugs, cheat on their wives, don't always obey the law, run red lights, drive drunk, are lazy, are on welfare, use food stamps, are takers, steal from the city, state and government, smoke crack, smoke drugs, do cocaine, beat their wives and girlfriends and sexually molest and physically abuse their children more than anyone else in America, that white men have a lot of sex with Black prostitutes, graze cattle on federal land and don't pay, are uncivilized, ignorant and uneducated.

Black Americans don't believe that there will be a race war, that the government and the laws will protect us. I would ask the many, many dozens of extinct Native American tribes, who were massacred by White men, what they thought about that. But then they have been extinct for a very long time and the few millions of Native Americans who are left and living on reservations, I won't bother asking them what they think about that.

****

Remember this is the same exact white man who killed off the Neanderthal man and a few other species of early man in Europe around twenty thousand to forty thousand years ago. White people don't know that all Black people think that 70% of White people are ignorant, trashy, stupid, uneducated and barbaric, especially Republican politicians.

Not one of the murderers that I grew up with, is more horrific and heinous than 70% of white people in the United States of America and their forefathers.

Not one person, murderer or thief, that I write about is worse than the many liars, cheats and thieves in the United States Congress

And so even the 30% have to suffer for the sins of their forefathers........
There are White people who love to help the countries of color in the Middle East, Africa, India, hell the world, and try to repair what their

48

ancestors have done, but white people destroyed so much and brought so much horror and poverty to these countries that even the 30% cannot seem to undo this wrong. And since white people in America all lump themselves together as one people, they can't have it both ways. Enjoying the rights and privileges stolen and forged through the massacre of millions of Native Americans and the horrors of American Black slavery and still want to be friends with people of color in America and the world.

America could be a great nation if it truly treated and educated all of its people equally. America could be a truly great nation if 70% of the White people did not live in it. Which means the greatness of America is in its people and the change only they can bring to it. 70% of the White people in America make it a bad place for everyone.

70% of White America could give one shit about black Americans' books, culture or lives. What they do care about is keeping African Americans unemployed, living in inhumane conditions, in poverty and working menial jobs for them.

After careful study and research, I have found that 70% of white people either hate me, dislike me and my culture, wish I didn't exist, want me to go back to Africa, think that I am not human, and if there were not hundreds of laws to prevent it, would castrate me, burn me, cut my dick off and lynch me.

I have come to the stupendous conclusion that no matter what, no African American child born in America, in the Ghetto, will ever have the equal footing to compete with any white child born in the United States of America, simply because the cards are stacked against them from birth and the enormous wealth of White America will prevail and keep the lie of equality non-existing.

9/11 may have been when terrorism came to the United States of America massively, but African Americans have been living in terrorism from White people in this country for over three hundred years, although 9/11 was horrific, so is the horrific treatment that Black people have undergone in America for centuries. White people are always questioning our patriotism, and so they should, and so they know, why they should.

No understanding of what money and currency means, no understanding of America finance, of Wall Street, of stocks and bonds, of what makes America work, because America doesn't really want Black people to know how America really works. White Americans make fun of how we talk, but we are not from the European language based on the Latin Phonetics, we are originally from the Languages of Africa. African Americans are just two, three or four steps removed from slaves who were bred as cattle, with no regard for them as humans, who survived the horrific, disgusting White people they had to encounter. And still we endured and we survived.

We live side by side in America watching on TV the privileges and entitlements of White people and still in the tens of millions we are cast adrift in our ghettos and housing projects to live and die in poverty, hunger and pain, until we are shot down dead, jailed or die in shit.

****

But America has too many poor Black people, too many poor White people, too many people living in poverty, with no proper housing, no proper jobs, no dignity, no proper education, no proper skills, living and dying in violence, killing one another, murdering, raping and preying upon the helpless, because poverty breeds contempt and hate for one another.

Who would have thought that the stink of poverty, the degradation of poverty, the humiliation of poverty, the corruption of poverty would still abide in these United States of America, a country where trillions of dollars are spent on other countries by the 70% of White people who actually rule America?

America goes to great lengths to hide African Americans' accomplishments in science, technology, math and space. We can never be smart or be heroes in America, unless we are entertaining white people. We can never be people who save and care for other people. Only White people can be heroes. Only White people can be shown as heroes. Only White people can go down in history year after year as this nation's heroes. Except for Martin Luther King, Jr., average American Black heroes unless they are athletes and entertainers get lost in American history. Case in point.......Jason Thomas.

****

JASON THOMAS

SOME INFORMATION FROM THE INTERNET

On the day following the September 11, 2001 World Trade Center attacks, 11 people were rescued from the fallen twin towers' rubble, including six firefighters and three police officers. One woman was rescued from the rubble, near where a West Side Highway pedestrian bridge had been.

An African American, former U.S. Marines Sergeant Jason Thomas discovered and saved two of them. Along with Staff Sergeant Dave Karnes, Sergeant Jason Thomas pulled out alive two Port Authority Police Department Officers, John McLoughlin and Will Jimeno, after they had spent nearly 24 hours beneath 30 feet of rubble. Their rescue was later portrayed in the Oliver Stone film, World Trade Center. The actor portraying Sergeant Jason Thomas was played by a white actor.

So no matter how they cleaned it up. No matter how much the producers of that film apologized to Sergeant Jason Thomas. Forever and always, til the end of time, long after Sergeant Jason Thomas is dead, for the next two hundred years of commemorating 9/11, that film footage alone will make sure that nobody will remember that an African American man was one of the major heroes of the 9/11 attacks on America and the World Trade Center.

This is just one of thousands of incidents in American History where a Black man's presence, heroism or invention, his very presence has been wiped clean of any historic value by the White media or the White system. It is impacted in the White American mindset that no African American can be a hero or anything unless he is in sports or entertainment. Meaning a Black man has to be entertaining White people to be considered somebody of importance.

THE BACK STORY

NEW YORK (AP) — *For years, authorities wondered about the identity of a U.S. Marine who appeared at the World Trade Center on Sept. 11, 2001, helped find a pair of police officers buried in the rubble, then vanished.*

Even the producers of the new film chronicling the rescue, World Trade Center, couldn't locate the mystery serviceman, who had given his name only as Sergeant Thomas.

51

The puzzle was finally solved when one Jason Thomas, of Columbus, Ohio, saw a TV commercial for the movie as he relaxed on his couch.

His eyes widened as he saw two Marines with flashlights, hunting for survivors atop the smoldering ruins.

"That's us. That's me!" thought Thomas, who lived in Long Island during the attacks and now works as an officer in Ohio's Supreme Court.

Thomas, 32, hesitantly re-emerged last week to recount the role he played in the rescue of Port Authority police officers Will Jimeno and Sgt. John McLoughlin, who were entombed beneath 20 feet of debris when the twin towers collapsed.

Back in New York to speak of his experience and visit family, Thomas provided the AP with photographs of himself at ground zero. As further proof of his identity, the movie's producer, Michael Shamberg, said Thomas and Jimeno have spoken by phone and shared details only the two of them would know.

Thomas, who had been out of the Marine Corps about a year, was dropping his daughter off at his mother's Long Island home when she told him planes had struck the towers.

He retrieved his Marine uniform from his truck, sped to Manhattan and had just parked his car when one of the towers collapsed. Thomas ran toward the center of the ash cloud.

"Someone needed help. It didn't matter who," he said. "I didn't even have a plan. But I have all this training as a Marine, and all I could think was, 'My city is in need.'"

Thomas bumped into another ex-Marine, Staff Sergeant, David Karnes, and the pair decided to search for survivors.

Carrying little more than flashlights and an infantryman's shovel, they climbed the mountain of debris, skirting dangerous crevasses and shards of red-hot metal, calling out "Is anyone down there? United States Marines!"

It was dark before they heard a response. The two crawled into a deep pit to find McLoughlin and Jimeno, injured but alive.

Jimeno would spend 13 hours in the pit before he was pulled free. Thomas stayed long enough to see him come up, but left due to exhaustion before

McLoughlin, who remained pinned for another nine hours, was retrieved.

Thomas said he returned to ground zero every day for another 2½ weeks to pitch in, then walked away and tried to forget.

"I didn't want to relive what took place that day," he said.

Shamberg said he apologized to Thomas for an inaccuracy in the film: Thomas is black, but the actor cast to portray him, William Mapother, is white. Filmmakers realized the mistake only after production had begun, Shamberg said.

Thomas laughed and gently chided the filmmakers, then politely declined to discuss it further. "I don't want to shed any negativity on what they were trying to show," he said.

As for his story, Thomas said he is gradually becoming more comfortable telling it.

"It's been like therapy," he said.

****

Jason Thomas was, as is the case with a lot of Black men, too forgiving of white people. He should have sued the film company for millions of dollars. Because he didn't his heroism and bravery as being the only person in American History to have pulled and saved two people on what is and will be the most memorialized and memorable day in American History, will be forgotten. And so as the years go on and on television year after year all you will see are White heroes from that day and time. The fact that an African American, a Black man was a hero who pulled out two people after the towers fell, will be forgotten forever.

And that's why the truth will never be told about the positive things that President Barack Obama did for America, for Americans, and his legacy in history will only show that he was a failed president, although he was one of the best and greatest American Presidents in American history.

53

CHAPTER 7

UNDER SEIGE IN BLACK AMERICA

Our Black communities in America have been under siege since slavery ended and we began to form our own towns and communities in America. We have been under siege and attacked by White America for one hundred and fifty years as free people. A declaration of war by the White people of America has been waged against Black people in America for two hundred and forty years. These arrogant White people were coming to all the dark countries of the world bringing death and racism.

From the 1500's to the 1970's the number one terrorists in the world were the White people of Western Europe and America, and they wonder why most countries and people of color around the world hate them. The problem is these people from Western Europe and America went to other shores all over the world and didn't see the people as human beings. It's a genetic disease that White people have, that says nobody else is equal to you, or better than you.

The Western European and American, African Atlantic Slave Trade Holocaust destroyed West Africa and all of Africa, causing the rape, death and cultural destruction of hundreds and hundreds of millions of African men, women and children, and lasted five hundred years. The German, Jewish Holocaust caused the death of six million Jewish men, women and children, and lasted six years.

****

America is a fraud. It says that everyone can succeed, no matter who you are. Well every regular and average African American man, woman and child in America, every pimp, gangster and hustler that I lived with, grew up with, survived with, and write about in *The Autobiography of an American Ghetto Boy*, knows that the playing field isn't even. That the deck has been stacked against African Americans from birth and knows that saying is not true.

The men and women of the '50's' and "60's' that I write about saw the regular and average black man humiliated regularly with no decent jobs, just menial labor work; so they determined early in life, that they could do better, not working for the white man and those with an entrepreneurial spirit started their own businesses and the only business available for a lot of these men and women was The Streets, The Life. And in that way they could at least have a chance at making a large amount of money at one time in their hands, rather than the crumbs the White Man and White society threw at the regular, average Black Man. Being a second generation gangster I saw the futility of it all, that the streets only got you jailed, or killed by the police, or by the streets. And because of a few very exceptional men and women I met in Boston and because I traveled out of the ghetto at an early age I met many more exceptional Black men and women who would show me another way, and so I survived and thrived.

America has a rich and wonderful history from which we as African Americans have been excluded and cannot fully enjoy.

****

All Black people need psychiatric help because of having to live with and work with White people. All White people need psychiatric help because they know their White privilege and entitlement comes from the murder, rape, enslavement, segregation and ostracism of Black people in American society.

The White American with the use of his guns and cannons, gave himself the best of everything, the best land, free land, stolen and taken by the most brutal and uncivilized methods possible all over the United States of America. The Native American was given back by the White man, the worst land. The Black man, 'til this day', was given the worst of everything with no land, no nothing.

All over America land, the best land, taken from the Indian man, land, stolen land, the white man gave himself the best land. The black man got no land, got nothing, before or after slavery, got nothing, but the white man always falsely claiming and lying that African Americans and the African American communities are takers and take everything. The White man takes everything with the use of his guns and cannons, including the Black man's culture, our music, taking our rap music, but don't march with us, looks at us like we're nothing, while they take everything, our spirits, our manhood, while we can't do nothing, because of their guns and cannons.

The White men were treated wonderfully wherever they went, until the word spread that they brought death, disease, murder, rape and massacre with them. Only when they had taken everything and killed everyone, could they then be benevolent and put into reservations and ghettos those who survived. The legacy of White American slavery, segregation and reservations is Black and Native American institutional and generational poverty. White supremacy is nothing but the white man showing Black people and other cultures who is in charge, who the boss is, who's really in charge of America. White people need to feel in charge of Black people.

The most natural thing in the world, the number one thing that a man does, is look at a woman. I'm thinking about the millions of young African and African American young men who were beaten, tortured, lynched, burnt, castrated, shot and killed, dead in the street for looking at White women. While White American men and White Western European men with their guns and cannons, not only looked at, but, repeatedly raped and sexually abused Black women for five hundred years of slavery and its aftermath and received no punishment and have never had to atone for their sins, ever. White men are the most profound mass murderers and serial rapists to ever walk the face of the Planet Earth.

AN INVESTIGATION AND STUDY OF
THE WHITE PEOPLE OF AMERICA AND
WESTERN EUROPE

VOLUME TWO

THE ORIGINS AND STUDY OF RACISM

CHAPTER 1

WHITE EVOLUTION

And so after 100,000 years down to 60,000 years ago, our brothers came home to Africa, but they did not recognize us anymore as their brothers, because they had mutated into something else, with White skin, stringy hair, thin lips, hard long noses and eyes of color. They had mutated to fit into the landscape of the white, cold land of Europe, the ice ages, where they had been living for 60-100,000 years.

They had mated with another humanoid called Neanderthal man and a lesser humanoid named Denisovans. Their noses had become thinner in order to breathe better and let less cold air into their bodies and lungs. Their lips had become thinner after thousands of centuries of pulling their lips in and back from the cold, thus protecting their lips from literally freezing off. And their skin turned white in order to fit in with the environment and in order to hide from the many beasts who wanted to eat them, and to hide better from other stone-age men like themselves. (See insert—Stone Age Hunter Had Blue Eyes and Dark Skin)

The cold made them a hard and violent thing, who's first thought was to kill whatever it encountered, eventually they mutated fully into what we call a Cro-Magnum man or a Caucasian.

And so they came back to Africa, at first to trade, and when there were skirmishes between the European (Portuguese and Spanish at first) and Africans it was on equal footing because both cultures were fighting with swords and spears and the Europeans could not conquer these Africans. The Greeks had tried and failed, the Romans had tried and for the most part failed, but by the 13th Century the Europeans had discovered gun powder from China and always war- minded they invented weapons that could fire a projectile and by the 14th Century they were pretty proficient at it and had developed a number of weapons, each one more horrendous in its ability to maim, destroy and kill other human beings.

By the time Columbus so-called discovered the New World, the Americas, they landed with guns and cannons, and when the Western European Portuguese and Spanish people came back to West Africa to trade, they came with guns and cannons, weapons that the Africans did not have; and by the time this mutated White thing from the cold of Europe was through, he would be the cause of Africa and hundreds of millions of African lives being changed through the use of their guns, cannons and diseases.

And this White savage would in turn, torture, rape, murder, massacre and enslave whole nations, whole cities, whole villages, whole countries of people of color, worldwide. All that death in order to expand and fulfill their greed for power, land, gold and slaves. For five hundred years this White savage subjugated the original man in Africa, Australia, South America, The Caribbean Islands, The Pacific Islands, North America with the horror and stench of hundreds of millions of deaths, all because of their greed for land, gold, silver, and power.

Whole nations of these primitive, barbaric, vicious white monkeys descended with the horrors of their psychotic desires and thirst for blood, rape and death on so-called uncivilized African and people of color throughout the world; people of the earth, farmers and laborers, people of the lakes, seas and oceans, fishermen; and slaughtered and enslaved them for profit, for greed, for their sexual desires. For their and their children's wealth and took these gentle people's lands and countries for their own and turned the people against one another, turned them into who they were and hated and then despised the people for what they had done to them.

And mind you all this was done in the name of their children and their children's, children, and their children's, children, and their children's, children, so that their children's, children, could rule the world into perpetuity; and it has worked, hasn't it! All that blood and death so that White people could have everything, rule the world, and Black and Brown people have nothing.

****

What happened to early man was that the further north he walked out of Africa, stayed and lived, after tens of thousands of centuries in northern Europe the whiter his skin mutated. Eventually somewhere in Sweden, Scandinavia and Russia his eyes mutated to blue eyes and eventually mutated to other color variations. The closer early man stayed to Africa, the less his skin and eyes changed as, in the Portuguese, Spanish, Sicilians,

Greeks and Italians whose skin to this day is darker, for the most part, then Northern Western Europeans.

Which is interesting, because the darker European, the Spanish and Portuguese with the most African genes, returned to Africa and created more horror and barbaric conditions for Africans than any Western European had up to the 15th and 16th centuries.

Whole countries became full of millions of lighter skinned Africans and their descendants, because of the wholesale and continual rape of captured African women and slaves by Portuguese, Spanish and Western European sub-human men during the 15th, 16th, 17th, 18th and 19th centuries. With in-breeding, whole countries to this very day, Cape Verde, Cuba, Santa Domingo, Brazil, Puerto Rico, Jamaica, and many, many others are populated and run by the lighter skinned descendants of the Western European rapists of female slaves.

****

Stone-Age Hunter Had Blue Eyes and Dark, African Skin

A European stone-age hunter's wisdom tooth has revealed that he had an unusual mix of racial traits – dark, African skin, curly brown hair and blue eyes.

Preliminary DNA analysis of the exceedingly well-preserved 7,000-year-old skeleton, dubbed Brana-1, has overturned ideas about the descent of modern Europeans.

Although the hunter's closest modern-day relatives live in Sweden and Finland, the genes for his skin color are African.

Previously, scientists thought that fair skin evolved as people moved to northern latitudes, allowing them to absorb more sunlight for the production of vitamin D.

"This guy had to be darker than any modern European, but we don't know how dark," said Carlos Lalueza-Fox of the Institute of Evolutionary Biology (IBE) in Barcelona.

The mutation for blue eyes, a change in the HERC2 gene, is thought to have first appeared around the Black Sea 10,000 years ago and then gradually moved west. Because the gene is recessive, blue-eyed people must have two copies, one from each parent. Remains of the hunter and another human were discovered by cavers in Brana-Arintero, a deep, complex cavern in the Cantabrian Mountains near Leon, Spain, in 2006. The constant cool temperature in the cave, 1,500 metres above sea level, protected the remains from bacteria.

Excavated by Julio Manuel Vidal Encinas, an archaeologist with the Council of Castilla y Leon, they were carbon dated to the Mesolithic era, which in Northwest Europe lasted from 10,000 to 5,000 years ago.

****

And so, the White Western European nations and later the United States descended into Africa like the vermin they were and destroyed, raped and plundered its most precious natural resource; its people—the farmers, the builders, the irrigation builders, the human beings who lived there, Africa's mothers, fathers and children.

Many, many, many, centuries before the Western European people began killing people of color around the world, they were killing each other by the tens of thousands. It was not unusual for a hundred thousand people to be killed on European battlefields. In fact, these people worshiped death and killing. They worshiped the art of killing, boys and men were taught to kill and to be worshiped for their skill at killing. Killing people is what the European mind set did best. The White man, with his guns and cannons, became the best killer on the face of the earth, a treacherous and deceitful killer.

A killer who lied and schemed over others to take their land, riches and to kill them. They spent centuries doing this to one another. They hated themselves and anyone unlike them, as much as they had hated the nobles in Europe who enslaved them as serfs and peasants

By the beginning of the last century they began World War One. Millions of Europeans were killed and many more millions of lives destroyed and then World War Two where over one hundred million men, woman and children were killed and many more millions of lives destroyed forever.

So for the Western European and the White American to kill hundreds of millions of Africans and millions of African Americans, as well as tens of millions of people of color throughout the world for the last six hundred years meant nothing to them. African Americans in the United States of America should know that this is not personal. This is who the majority of White people have always been, killers, who kill for greed and power. The White American will do whatever is necessary to show his power over us, that he is more powerful, smarter, more intelligent and has the power of life and death over people of color in every way. White supremacy is nothing but the white man showing Black people who is in charge, who the boss is, who's really in charge of America. White people need to feel in charge of Black people.

The Western European and the White American is the cruelest, most horrific killer of human beings to ever walk the earth. Whenever we meet or see a White man we should all just spit on him for the deaths of our millions of ancestors.

Western Europeans invented racism, they brought it to America in 1632. But White Americans bought, and sold it all over the world. White Americans turned racism and life in America into a barbaric, uncivilized and cruel journey for hundreds of millions of African Americans from 1776 to the present.

CHAPTER 2

WHITE DEATH, DESTRUCTION AND ENSLAVEMENT

In Western Europe there were hundreds of cultures and sub-cultures, from the English, French, Italian, Dutch, Spanish, and German. In America all of these cultures became known as White people or the White Race. Their combined one and only enemy is Black people.

From 1492 until now, the Western European, English, Dutch, Spanish, Portuguese, French, German, Belgians, Italians, who became known as White People in America. Humiliated, degraded, murdered, raped, with guns and cannons, hundreds and hundreds and hundreds of millions of Africans, African Americans, Native Americans, Incas, Mayans, Chinese, Japanese, Hawaiians, Tahitians, in fact every person of color in the world, and destroyed us psychologically, emotionally and physically. Yet today we're supposed to smile and say you forgive them, and you forgive their children's, children, children, because you see they won America and the world. They have everything they want. So now they can be your friend, and after their forefathers murdered, slaughtered and extinguished our ancestors, for the benefit of their future generations, their children now want to be your friend and smile and laugh with you and be your friend.

My black ancestors, my forefathers were bathed in blood, sweat and shit. So that the White inheritors of their forefathers' greed and quest for gold, land, power and money could play with their iPads and be friends with us. We are never to mention that their power, their inventiveness, their iPads came from the horrific rape and enslavement of my forefathers.

And see it worked. All that 'we're doing this for our children' worked for White people. Whether they had to murder, massacre, rape, steal, enslave others to get their wealth, land, and own the world, they did; and now their children, and great, great, great, great grandchildren have reaped the benefits; and now own the world and now want to be nice to us.

What I have written is not just how I think, it is how and what every single Black man and woman knows and thinks. Most won't or can't tell White people this and have to try to be friends with White people because they believe that White people are powerful, hold the keys to the kingdom, and that they can't get ahead without White people loving them. The rapper Common now comes to mind.

****

After World War One and World War Two the European Western and Eastern European countries were sick of war and still are. But America is not. White American knows that the only way to make sure that their children and grandchildren continue to have everything, is to keep subjugating everyone. That is just one of the reasons that they don't like President Barack Obama, because they don't believe that he has White people's best interest at heart. Which is to make sure that White people stay the leaders of the world. They don't believe that any Black person has the best interest of this country and should not and cannot lead America. They believe that President Obama is a mistake that should never be repeated.

The one blessed thing for all that horror that the White man has inflicted on Black people and people of color throughout the world, is that every last one of these people's forefathers and foremothers who participated in every aspect of the horrors of slavery and the massacre of the native Americans is now residing in hell with their everlasting souls and spirits.

Wherever they went in the world with their filthy ships and filthy diseases, Western Europeans and Americans brought death, destruction and enslavement. They thought that the people of color were worshiping them, because they were something special. The fact is that no one had ever seen this type of man before and because their skin was more different than anyone had ever seen before; most of the people on earth, were people of color, the people saw White people as a thing of curiosity, much the same way they saw an albino and wanted to touch their skin, their hair and get to know this type of man.

Some cultures thought that they were gods from another world and worshipped them. Much like aliens who come to Earth and say that they come in peace and then turn on you with their superior weapons and filthy diseases and begin to conquer you and destroy you and your culture. You might at first think that the aliens were gods.

70% of the White people in America will say, "Oh there goes another one, using the race card again. But what 30% of the White people in

America know is that racism is a European invention, a white people invention. Western Europeans and White Americans went all over the world spreading disease, death and racism, all over the world, from Japan to China, to Australia, from Africa to India, from South America to the Pacific Islands, from North America to the West Indies, they enslaved the populations, brought death, disease and inhuman and cruel treatment to all, and to all they brought their superior attitude and need for White Supremacy and quest for power and greed.

The real America has no jobs for poor African Americans. There are few major Black corporations. No real land was given to African Americans. 98% of slaves received nothing but their freedom and were instantly placed in institutional and generational poverty, allowing African Americans to stay poor, generation after generation.

White people are constantly making fun of us and saying we are nothing, we are lazy and need to pull ourselves up, steering away from the real problem which is to keep Black people poor.

These same White people are always talking about we should go back to Africa. Well if these lazy White motherfuckers had of been willing to plant their own tobacco, pick their own cotton, farm their own rice, build their own country, we wouldn't have had to have been here.

CHAPTER 3

WARRIORS

We have to remember that although some White people seem civilized today, that everything that they have, everything, all the power, privilege, land, entitlement, education, that they have, everything, is based on the barbaric, cruel and inhumane treatment by their forefathers towards Africans, African Americans, Native Americans, Hispanic Americans, Australian Aborigines, Asian Americans, Iñupiat, Yupik, Aleut, Eyak, Tlingit, Haida, Tsimshian, Eskimo Americans and Hawaiian Americans.

Every White person in the United States of America, for the last 365 years, has been the beneficiary of untold wealth and land and education and power and privilege and entitlement, through the murder, massacre, rape, enslavement, cultural destruction, distortion, segregation and isolation of African Americans and Native Americans.

Black people work in an environment of racism when working with White people. President Barack Obama works in an environment of racism while trying to work with White people in the United States Congress and Senate of the United States of America. The goal of the White leadership is to make President Obama look so incompetent that no one will ever vote for a Black man in America again.

The United States Congress and Government gives billions of dollars to other countries, cultures, corporations and banks, while poor Black and White Americans starve, live like shit, and have nothing.

Someone once said that we should spit on every White person that we see, meet or talk to. That might be hard, to spit on every White person that we see, because some White people don't deserve that and have proven themselves worthy of our respect. But since every White person has had a sense of entitlement because of the horrific behavior of their ancestors, we still always have to remember that every White person in America has benefited through the laws of slavery and Jim Crow; through the murder, killings, rape, enslavement, union lockouts, job lockouts and segregation of Black People.

African American teenagers, men and women have served, been wounded and died in every war that the United States has fought. From the Revolutionary War to the Iraq and Afghanistan Wars.

African Americans have made, helped make, and shaped policies in the United States that have benefited hundreds and hundreds of millions of Americans, from the nineteenth century to the Affordable Care Act. (Obama Care) Policies and laws that will help hundreds and hundreds of millions of Americans in the future.

African American music; Spirituals, The Blues, Jazz and Rhythm and Blues, the only real American music, is responsible for Rock and Roll, Rock, Hard Rock and Pop Music, and the trillions and trillions and trillions of dollars made from the music all over the world, most of it to White people.

****

African Americans have invented thousands of inventions that have made life better for hundreds and hundreds of millions of Americans through over one hundred and fifty years of inventions and will help hundreds and hundreds of millions more Americans in the future. African Americans have been involved in every facet of American life helping to make America a better place to live for almost four hundred years, and yet we can still be shot down dead in the street for the most minimum offence, vilified, scorned, laughed at, denied, attacked and hated by 70% of White Americans, who know nothing about us or our history in America.

I'm assuming that most of you who read this list will Google these few inventors of the many, many thousands of Black inventors and inventions, as you should. Most of the inventors listed here are from 19th century America. Enjoy the read. Oh by the way. One of the inventors listed below Benjamin Banneker, a freed slave, also helped in the planning and design of Washington, DC, including the White House.

Black Inventors and their Inventions List

air conditioning unit Frederick M. Jones July 12, 1949
almanac Benjamin Banneker Approx 1791
auto cut-off switch Granville T. Woods January 1, 1839
auto fishing devise G. Cook May 30, 1899
automatic gear shift Richard Spikes February 28, 1932
baby buggy W.H. Richardson June 18, 1899
bicycle frame L.R. Johnson October 10, 1899
biscuit cutter A.P. Ashbourne November 30, 1875
blood plasma bag Charles Drew Approx. 1945
cellular phone Henry T. Sampson July 6, 1971
chamber commode T. Elkins January 3, 1897
clothes dryer G. T. Sampson June 6, 1862
curtain rod S. R. Scratton November 30, 1889
curtain rod support William S. Grant August 4, 1896
door knob O. Dorsey December 10, 1878
door stop O. Dorsey December 10, 1878
dust pan Lawrence P. Ray August 3, 1897
egg beater Willie Johnson February 5, 1884
electric lamp bulb Lewis Latimer March 21, 1882
elevator Alexander Miles October 11, 1867
eye protector P. Johnson November 2, 1880
fire escape ladder J. W. Winters May 7, 1878
fire extinguisher T. Marshall October 26, 1872
folding bed L. C. Bailey July 18, 1899
folding chair Brody & Surgwar June 11, 1889
fountain pen W. B. Purvis January 7, 1890
furniture caster O. A. Fisher 1878
gas mask Garrett Morgan October 13, 1914
golf tee T. Grant December 12, 1899
guitar Robert F. Flemming, Jr. March 3, 1886
hair brush Lydia O. Newman November 15, 18--
hand stamp Walter B. Purvis February 27 1883
horse shoe J. Ricks March 30, 1885
ice cream scooper A. L. Cralle February 2, 1897
improv. sugar making Norbet Rillieux December 10, 1846
insect-destroyer gun A. C. Richard February 28, 1899
ironing board Sarah Boone December 30, 1887
key chain F. J. Loudin January 9, 1894

lantern Michael C. Harvey August 19, 1884
lawn mower L. A. Burr May 19, 1889
lawn sprinkler J. W. Smith May 4, 1897
lemon squeezer J. Thomas White December 8, 1893
lock W. A. Martin July 23, 18--
lubricating cup Ellijah McCoy November 15, 1895
lunch pail James Robinson 1887
mail box Paul L. Downing October 27, 1891
mop Thomas W. Stewart June 11, 1893
motor Frederick M. Jones June 27, 1939
peanut butter George Washington Carver 1896
pencil sharpener J. L. Love November 23, 1897
phone transmitter Granville T. Woods December 2, 1884
record player arm Joseph Hunger Dickenson January 8, 1819
refrigerator J. Standard June 14, 1891
riding saddles W. D. Davis October 6, 1895
rolling pin John W. Reed 1864
shampoo headrest C. O. Bailiff October 11, 1898
spark plug Edmond Berger February 2, 1839
stethoscope Imhotep Ancient Egypt
stove T. A. Carrington July 25, 1876
straightening comb Madam C. J. Walker Approx 1905
street sweeper Charles B. Brooks March 17, 1890
thermostat control Frederick M. Jones February 23, 1960
traffic light Garrett Morgan November 20, 1923
tricycle M. A. Cherry May 6, 1886
typewriter Burridge & Marshman April 7, 1885

CHAPTER 4

UGLY WHITE GHOSTS

A real ghetto in America, every Black Ghetto, Housing Project and Community in America, is full of emotionally, sexually, mentally, physiologically, and physically beaten down people, who have given up on life and jobs. There are no jobs for African Americans in the ghetto, except the most menial jobs at fast food outlets like McDonalds. In the real ghettos and housing projects of America there is no life except extreme poverty and victimization.

As in every culture there is evil and there is good. Some of the people in my life that I write about in my autobiography, *The Autobiography of an American Ghetto Boy,* were just plain evil, ignorant and stupid, and it had nothing to do with slavery, racism, segregation or non-inclusion. Just as most people of every culture are seemingly good, some people are just plain stupid and evil.

But, let me make this very clear, the most fundamentally cruel and evil people on the face of the earth have been the ugly white ghosts. They and their ancestors, once they had the use of guns and cannons, have been responsible for the murder, cultural, economic, physical and emotional destruction of hundreds and hundreds and hundreds and hundreds of millions of people of color throughout the world.

When I was a child we used to call White people *Ugly White Ghosts,* because that's what they looked like to us. After a long while and as I got older, I began to see that they thought of themselves as beautiful and perfect; and not only that, I found out later that because their skin was white, they actually thought that they were better and smarter than anyone else on the planet earth. What they didn't tell anybody was that they were killers, who would kill anyone for the most depraved and unscrupulous reasons. Which always ended up being world domination and greed, oh, and let us not forget it was all for their children.

Well, after many years of study and research, I found that they were neither beautiful nor were they perfect, in fact most of the world's ills were caused through their mistakes, lies and deceits. I found that these people were born killers and were genetically programmed to hate anyone who did not look like them, act like them or worship like them and that would include each other.

****

America and its guns and cannons wasn't the only country to participate in the massacre and slavery of Africans and the massacre of Native South, Central, Caribbean and North American People. Every Western European country including: Great Britain, France, Germany, Belgium, Spain, Portugal, The Netherlands and Italy participated in the enslavement, rape, massacre, colonization and pillaging of Africa and the Americas' natural resources and the cultural, physical, mental and emotional destruction of its African and Native American people.

All of Africa was destroyed by Western Europe and the United States of America during the Atlantic Slave Trade and European Colonization. To this very day the countries hardest hit by White European countries, America, and its corporations, institutions and people are: Benin, Burkina Faso, Cape Verde, The Ivory Coast, Gambia, Ghana, Guinea, Guinea-Bissau, Liberia, Mali, Niger, Nigeria, Senegal, Sierra Leone, Togo, South Africa, The Central Republic of Africa and Angola, in fact all of Africa is still sub-standard, impoverished, and corrupt because of the extraordinary horrific and degrading conditions of the Atlantic Slave Trade and Western European Colonization.

Canada was one of the few White nations that did not participate in colonization of an African country and did not participate in the slave trade. In fact, Canada became a refuge for escaped American Slaves and thus is a nation not eroded and condemned, unlike the United States of America, with the hate, stench and brutality of slavery and its descendants, both white and black.

African and African American slavery provided the capital which financed America and Europe's industrial revolution. This would include the advancement and growth of modern technology, the computer revolution and globalization, which is the basis of all futuristic scientific findings in modern and all material solutions for many of man's challenges.

The fact is that if Africans had not been abducted by the use of guns and cannons against their will and made into slaves, The United States and the Western European powers would not be anywhere near as economically strong and powerful as they are today.

AN INVESTIGATION AND STUDY OF THE
WHITE PEOPLE OF AMERICA AND
WESTERN EUROPE

VOLUME THREE

AN INVESTIGATION AND STUDY OF THE
BLACK PEOPLE OF AMERICA
POOR, BLACK AND GHETTOIZED

CHAPTER 1

THE BLACK COMMUNITY AND POST-TRAUMATIC STRESS DISORDER

WHITE AMERICA DEMONIZES AFRICAN AMERICANS AS ANIMALS JUST SO THEY CAN PRACTICE RACISM, SEGREGATION, DISCRIMINATION, INEQUALITY, POLICE INJUSTICE, POLITICAL INJUSTICE AND ECONOMIC INJUSTICE AGAINST BLACK AMERICANS.

Most poor African American children who live in or come from the real projects and ghettos of America, like Chicago, Los Angeles, Miami, St. Louis, Boston and hundreds of other American cities need psychiatric help for PTSD, depression, and mental illness. I believe there is no difference between the children living in the housing projects or ghettos of America than soldiers going off to war in World War One, World War Two, Vietnam, Iraq or Afghanistan.

Most poor people living in ghettos and housing projects live in a shell-shocked world where violence is an everyday occurrence, where death is common, where the most horrific aspects of sex and violence are synonymous with everyday living. When a White child commits atrocities in America it must be because he fell through the cracks and didn't get the mental help he so deserved. When a Black child commits horrific crimes and murder, it's because he's black and by birth is a brutal animal and gets life and forever in jail, where his or her abuse and life continues to be one long night in hell.

The White man taught us everything we know. How to disrespect ourselves, our women, our culture and our communities. How to kill each other, how to disrespect each other, how to hate each other, how to be jealous of each other, how to not support one another, how to be afraid of one another.

After 350 years of having to live with white people, we have become just like them in the way that they treated us, so do we treat one another. And that's why our Black ghettos, our communities are so full of hate. We sell each other drugs and death in the housing projects and in the ghetto. We are living the way the white man has made us in his image. Full of hate and loathing for one another, killing each other slowly with drugs, painfully with humiliation, and fast with guns and violence.

Every African American who was born, raised or has lived more than five years in the real projects or real urban or rural ghettos of America suffers from Post-Traumatic Stress Disorder. Every African American who lived through segregation in the south suffered from Post-Traumatic Stress Disorder. Every African American who lived through segregation in the north suffered from Post-Traumatic Stress Disorder. Every African American who marched for their civil rights in the south and north suffered from Post-Traumatic Stress Disorder. Every slave in the south or north suffered from Post- Traumatic Stress Disorder.

Every African American slave who was freed and walked to freedom in the south suffered from Post- Traumatic Stress Disorder. Every African American who lived through segregation in the south suffered from Post-Traumatic Stress Disorder. Every former slave who lived through reconstruction in the south suffered from Post-Traumatic Stress Disorder. Every African American, slave or otherwise who has lived or lives in White America to this very day, this very minute, this very second suffers from Post-Traumatic Stress Disorder and needs professional help. And that would include me.

Hundreds and hundreds of millions of African Slaves and African Americans have lived for the last three hundred and sixty-five years in America, being terrorized, living in trauma, humiliated and hated by White Americans and suffered and still suffers from Post-Traumatic Stress Disorder. This Post-Traumatic Stress Disorder has like intergenerational poverty, been passed down from generation to generation, it is a serious cultural and mental flaw and needs to be addressed by America.

****

If anyone needs proof of this, then you need look no further than our urban cities and prisons where millions of African Americans destroy one another every day in many horrendous and violent ways. Tens of thousands of inner city Black People in every major American City are self-medicating themselves with heroin, crack, cocaine, marijuana and alcohol. The drugs are provided by the......and take your pick... the

Government, the CIA, the Mafia, the Columbian Cartel, the Mexican Cartel, the White man, the drug man, the boogieman and the corner man. All of these entities are trying to destroy you and the community, all because you are poor, angry, helpless, homeless, jobless, no real money, no hope, no nothing. You got just enough to pay for your drugs and stay poor, black, hungry and angry, with nothing.

The thing is, at this point, is everyone who works or is trying to help people in the ghetto is suffering from PTSD and that would include the cops, the firemen, the paramedics, the community hospital health workers, the welfare system, and the city government. Everyone in or close to the ghetto has now become mentally and emotionally disabled.

But as the old laws against education for black people stated, "The White system needs a slave work force, and Black people are it". The prison system needs a criminal work force, and you're it. When you don't have an education or skill everyone profits except you. When you're in court everyone is making money, except you. When you're in prison, everyone is making money, except you. When you don't have an education or skill, everyone is making money, except you. The only thing you can do is work a slave job for minimum wages and be poor for the rest of your life or you can make money the street way and go to jail and or die violently.

****

Those are your choices when you are born and raised and live more than seventeen years in the housing projects or ghetto. When you don't have some type of job skill or education at something that somebody wants, those are your choices and remember rapping is not a job. Becoming a musician, playing piano or guitar can be a job and you can make money with those skills.

But rapping is not a job, and won't make you any money unless you can find a manager, an attorney, a publicist, an agent, a record company, a distributor and sell two million cd's and everybody in the world, promoters, agents, managers, record company makes real money off of you, and maybe some of that money will trickle down to you. On your next million seller you might make a lot of money unless you owe your manager, agent, record company even more money and then you will still make nothing.

So unless you are very lucky, your best bet is to get a scholarship, get an education or go into the military from high school while you're still working out life, unless you've already fucked up and didn't graduate or got locked up for doing something stupid, and now you have a felony and can't do shit. Those are your choices when you come from the real ghetto, from the real projects.

My advice is to simply stop doing stupid shit. Learn what's real, don't terrorize and disrespect your own community, your own brothers and sisters by selling them drugs and committing crimes against your own community, and don't forget, if you do crack or heroin or drugs like that, you will never get out. A drug addict can't live no more than five miles from his or her drug dealer and once again the white man will have you, since he's the one providing your drug dealer with the drugs so that you can be addicted. He's the one putting the crack pipe, zig zag papers and alcohol in the community so you can do some crime, commit a felony and get sent to prison where you can be a slave of the state for 3-5, 5-10, 10-20 or 20-life and then you will never get out, even if you're out you will live in poverty and be a slave hustling in the ghetto for the rest of your life, until you die violently or slowly.

Go to school, and no matter what, get some type of education or skill. If you are not going on to college, community college or have no academic or athletic scholarship to a University and you are seventeen or eighteen years old, you can still go into the United States Air Force, Navy, or Marines, and get out of the ghetto. Stop living off of your mother or grandmother and grow up while you get paid in the military. But get the fuck up out of the projects, the ghetto, they are death traps. Join the military, learn a job skill, meet a lot of girls, travel around the world and get paid while you are figuring it all out.

So, because I come from the real projects, the real ghetto, I can tell you this. Don't let the White system define you, don't let the ghetto define you, don't let the projects define you. Don't let them lock you in and have you thinking that the streets are your life, that, that corner defines you and you are locked in to poverty for the rest of your life. You can get out, you can escape, don't let those White people laws of red-lining and segregation define you. Segregation and red-lining still exists, but don't let it define you. Fight, be the hard bad-motherfucker you think you are, break out, before they trap you with a felony and then you can't go anywhere.

****

As I write about in my book, *The Autobiography of an American Ghetto Boy,* I was eighteen years old on the verge of stepping up to my first felony, gun in hand, and a voice whispered to me that I had been graduated from high school by a man who said I just had to swim four laps at the Boys Club, and that I didn't have to be at my mother's house anymore, that I didn't have to be in a gang anymore, that I didn't have to do crime anymore, that I could leave now. Then, God took my hand and rode with me on the bus down to the United States Air Force recruiting office and I began my journey out.

Remember this, the odds are that you are average, nothing special yet, because you have not defined yourself. The odds are that you don't have any money, no academic or athletic scholarship, can't get into college because you don't have the grades. You can't really rap or sing that good, no job, no real father, no real mother, no real education, no real social skills. You get high too much, you drink too much alcohol, you have no real girlfriends, just some sex, you're going nowhere and you're sixteen, seventeen, eighteen or nineteen. The solution isn't the drug game, that's the White man's trap. The solution is to get out.

The solution isn't crime, that's the White man's trap so he can send you to prison to be his slave. The solution isn't being sixteen, seventeen, eighteen, nineteen, twenty, twenty-one and terrorizing your community with your presence, that's the White man's trap to define you and keep you in poverty. The solution is to use the White man and his system and go to Community College and get an education and get some skills that can take you to the next level or go into the Military and have the United States of America pay for your education or job skill, and educate yourself with a skill that somebody will want and pay for.

What happens in the poor black communities of America where I am from is a form of genocide, suicide if you will. Where because of the daily, hourly, struggle to survive, to eat, to pay rent, to pay bills, to raise children in poverty, in fear, no jobs, and the degradation of being black and poor in America causes one to embrace the horrors of heroin, crack cocaine, weed and alcohol, which all live side by side with you in the form of liqueur stores and your community drug dealers who prey upon you day and night, and have the power to corrupt and destroy whole neighborhoods with prostitution, rape, petty and violent crimes.

They get their heroin, crack cocaine, weed and alcohol from the White man. The needles to shoot heroin come from the White man, the pipe used to smoke crack comes from the White man, the alcohol comes from the White man's liquor store, the papers and apparatus used to smoke weed come from the White man's stores. None of these items, the needles, the pipe, the papers, the alcohol, nor the liquor stores are owned by Black people or manufactured in the poor urban Black communities.

In fact, no one seems to know where the crack pipe is manufactured or how it miraculously appears in every Black community in America. Every major Black community in every poor Black city, town and village in America is surrounded by and under siege by liquor stores and drug dealers. They turn our children into alcoholics and drug and crack addicts, every day, across the country, from Boston to Los Angeles, by the thousands, every day.

****

Most of our African American leaders like Reverend Al Sharpton, National Action Network; Reverend Jesse Jackson, Operation Push; Ben Jealous, former NAACP, President/CEO; Corey Booker, Senator, New Jersey; and even Barack Obama, the President of the United States have attempted to help the poor and at risk children of this country through their words and example. The problem is that 99.9% of these leaders don't come from where these children come from...they haven't lived their lives, and aren't able to truly understand the dangers that are all around these children.

These leaders haven't lived day after day, night after night, year after year as children, with violence, poverty, degradation, drugs, and the horrors of prostitution, drug dealing, depravity and no hope all around them; with the stink of poverty all around them, the evil of poverty surrounding them, the stink of death all around them. The reason we don't have leaders coming from such an horrific place is that the majority of the people who come from this bad environment—bad parents, bad schools—living with no hope, are mentally, physically and emotionally unable to perform as leaders; or they're in jail, or they're on drugs, or they're on alcohol, or they're still living on the fringes of society in a bad condition in a bad way...in poverty.

These leaders did not come from dysfunctional and violent families and have no clue why one child will kill another child, one child will rape another child, one child will torture another child, one child will sell drugs to another child, one child will set another child on fire, one child will gang rape another child. They don't know that, that child has been beaten, abused, starved, raped and suffered from bad food and a bad education, year after year. They don't know that child has never been on vacation anywhere, no summer vacations to Disneyland, no summer home, no boat rides, no boat trips, no camping trips, no plays, no nothing.

These so-called leaders have no idea why these children act out in school, rob other children, destroy their communities, sell pussy, sell crack, sell PCP, sell heroin, pimp, prostitute and hustle. They do not understand that these children are bombarded by television and the outside world showing them wealthy beyond belief athletes, entertainers, and corporations, while they live in a world of trauma, violence, death, poverty and hunger; suffering every day from the effects of mental, physical and sexual abuse and yet they are expected to go to school and pretend that everything is okay, pretend that everything is normal, that they are living a normal American life; and expected to achieve in school where they are basically learning just how wonderful White men and women are. That they are just like some White kid from a middle or upper class home.

Our leaders need to work on changing American school curriculums in the African American community to match and better reflect that African American child's reality of self and self-esteem. Then maybe this country's Public Schools will be an interesting learning center for that child.

****

I have always felt that since slavery and colonialism was a global affair initiated and practiced by the Western European powers of the 15th, 16th, 17th, 18th and 19th Centuries and White North and South Americans of the 17th, 18th and 19th Centuries who committed horrendous atrocities that included rape, murder, enslavement and the displacement of tens of millions of Africans and African American slaves, that Africans and the freed descendants of slaves and that would include 95% of African Americans in the United States of America should petition for reparations in the Hundreds and Hundreds of Billions of dollars from the United Nations. African Americans should begin the process by declaring our American Urban Cities our ghettos, Third World Countries, and petition the United Nations for relief in the form of education, jobs and decent housing.

How to win against the White man when you're a child. Get a strong education and don't commit crimes against your community.

There are two problems with the Black community. Teenagers who never have a chance or reason to leave the community until they are shot, killed or go to jail; and police who do not come from Black communities. Our medical care is often secondary and third rate. When we are sick, we are often not believed and very often get misdiagnosed. All African American children want go to school, work and go to colleges, universities, and trade schools, but because of the extreme poverty, high unemployment and widespread cultural and community destruction, terror, trauma, and fear in our communities, they drop out.

Black on Black crime occurs because our major American cities are overrun with tens of thousands of poor, undereducated, hungry, degraded, unemployed, people all living on top of one another, preying on one another, living in poverty, the good people, the working class people, living with drug addicts and criminals of all types.

CHAPTER 2

SLAVERY AND SEGREGRATION REPARATIONS

Slavery, Segregation and White Male Oppression are the legacies that formed extreme poverty, high unemployment, and widespread cultural and community destruction in the African American community.

The United States Government, and its Corporations and Institutions who participated in Slavery, Segregation and Jim Crow in this country need to give reparations and an apology to all of the descendants of Slavery. Every African American person in this country needs to be given a free education at the career, trade or skill they desire by the United States Government and every Corporation and Institution in this country and that would mean Institutions like Harvard University and Corporations like New York Life should pay for this education and physiological therapy for African Americans.

This education would go a long way to help correct a self-destructive condition resulting from a black state of mind that was created during our forefathers' enslavement in America and the colonization by Western Europeans, with their guns and cannons, of West Africa, Africa and the all the darker peoples of the earth. This would help cleanse the horrendous conditions of life among poor Black people living in the housing projects and ghettos of the United States of America. A way of life that has emerged from White supremacy and the slave master mentality that is the vestige of a three century chattel slavery system in America, forcibly imposed upon Black people by the White people of today and their forefathers of yesterday, along with another century and a half of Jim Crow, segregation, discrimination, inequality, and injustice which continues to this day.

My belief is that every African American should be given a free economic and financial education in the higher education schools of America. A free education at the community colleges, colleges and universities of their choice from the age of seventeen—twenty-five and particularly at all of the schools that participated in the slave trade. America, the United States of America, say you're sorry and give some reparations, it would help still the pain and help create a new generation of confidence in America for African Americans

****

We as African Americans have been subjected to a level of murder, lynching's, burnings, cruel and inhumane treatment, lies, deception, disrespect, jealousy, treachery, betrayal, and sabotage from within America that no other culture, except the Native American has ever experienced, and still we succeed and our success always makes America better, and so it shall be and always will be, always and forever.

One of the major problems with African Americans is that we need to hear an apology from the United States Government for the mass enslavement and slaughter of African Americans and the mass slaughter of Native Americans in this country. If you live in America and your ancestors were of Western European heritage and came to America only one or two generations ago, then you are reaping the privileges and benefits of the horrors of African American slavery and the mass extermination of Native Americans.

Tens of millions of my fellow African American, brothers' and sisters' forefathers were cast adrift in the millions from the blood, sweat and bondage of slavery in the United States of America in 1865. Not knowing where they were, where they were from, who they were, where they were going or what they were; with no money, no land, no nothing; no wealthy cousin or rich father to see to them; no love for America, no food, no jobs, no education, no understanding of the white system of money; no understanding of the law, no understanding of land and power, no understanding of American government, no understanding of America, no real understanding of the White people who hated them.

Migrating all over America, North, West, East, anywhere but, the South, and somehow forming unions of oneness, of communities and businesses. We made a way out of no way and survived, even flourished, only to have filth, death and drugs rammed down our throats and still we continue to survive without the proper education and understanding of language and finance to fight it off.

Why reparations for the victims? The children's, children's, children's, children's, children's, children's, children's, children of genocide and the mass murder of hundreds of millions of Africans and African Americans; for slavery, slave trading, racial apartheid of housing and economic laws and the one hundred and fifty years of Jim Crow laws that caused economic, physical, emotional abuse, harm, suffering and crimes against humanity; to the entire African American community by the 70% of White people today who's father's, father's, father's, father's, father's, father's, father, committed these horrors and abuses against Africans and African Americans for the benefit of their children today.

****

In 2006, Brown University issued an extraordinary report detailing the university's relationship with the slave trade and acknowledged the deep, intertwined history of the slave trade and the university and the role slave labor played in the very construction of the school.

But Brown is hardly the only venerable university in the United States that is reckoning with its hidden legacy of slavery, practically every college and university founded during colonial-era America – Harvard University, William & Mary, Yale, Princeton, the University of Pennsylvania, Columbia, Brown, Rutgers, and Dartmouth, has a history of slavery to confront, and most older institutions of higher education in America were built on the back of slave labor. The first eight presidents of Princeton – then the College of New Jersey – were slave owners, and enslaved people lived in the presidents' houses and served the presidents and students.

In the evolution of the Harvard / Yale / Princeton faculties, and the founding moment of Yale, when the founding trustees gathered to plan out the organization and wrote the bylaws of the new school, they were accompanied by their slaves to that meeting. It was interesting to see how much these academic institutions depended upon enslaved people, but also on the broader economy of the slave trade.

Many of the founders of these universities became quite wealthy as merchants profiting off of the slave trade. When you think about Columbia or the University of Pennsylvania, or Dartmouth, you think of them as wealthy, historic institutions. But these were pretty lean institutions in the eighteenth century, when they were founded. They were local institutions. The ministers and local activists founded these schools turned to local sources of wealth, and in the mid-Atlantic and New England, that meant they often turned to families who made their fortunes in the Atlantic trade, and a significant proportion of that trade was in African slaves.

Harvard University turned to local merchants in the seventeenth century, many of whom were British suppliers who sent fish, for instance, south to the West Indies. The cheapest quality fish was what was sent down to feed the enslaved population of the West Indies. Not only did Harvard's New England backers have close ties to West Indian slavery, the school also followed these commercial networks south to seek out wealthy West Indian slave owners.

At Brown, when the original trustees were raising donations for the school, local residents of Providence and Newport donated cash, lumber, and other goods, and they donated the labor of their slaves. At the College of William and Mary, teams of slaves were used for the upkeep of various buildings, and the College actually held a fairly sizable population of slaves for use as campus servants, dedicated at times to specific buildings.

Some of the students at William and Mary brought slaves to campus with them. Eleazar Wheelock, the founder of Dartmouth, arrived in New Hampshire in 1770. He brought with him eight enslaved black people, and he wrote in his memoir about the early struggle to build the college. He wrote about the use of his slaves to help lay out the fields and raise some of the original structures of the college to get things going. He has several places in his memoirs about the things he'd assigned his slaves to do to improve the campus and expand his ability to take in students.

****

As I have stated before, the use of slave labor was highly prized in America, as slaves were the best builders and agriculturists in America.

Slave labor built the White House, Washington, DC and every major institution in every major city and state in America's Northeast, Mid-Atlantic and South between 1626 and 1865.

Without Benjamin Banneker, a freed slave, our nation's capital would not exist as we know it. After a year of work, a Frenchman hired by George Washington to design the capital, L'Enfant, stormed off the job, taking all the plans. Benjamin Banneker, placed on the planning committee at Thomas Jefferson's request, saved the project by reproducing from memory, in two days, a complete layout of the streets, parks, and major buildings, including the White House. Thus Washington, D.C. itself can be considered a monument to the genius of this great man.

CHAPTER 3

BLACK PEOPLE AND SLAVE REPARATIONS

Our forefathers have earned us reparation by their blood, sweat, tears and lives.

95% of the African American freed slaves in 1865 could not read, write or do any kind of math. It was against the law for the White man's property to read or write. If a slave was found to be able to read or write from 1650 - 1865, he or she could by the laws of the Southern States be subject to 100 lashes from the whip or death by hanging, castration, and being burnt alive.

President Barack Obama is a true African American. He is the embodiment and look of five hundred years of White men raping African women, he is the look of slavery in the United States, Europe, South America and the Caribbean. But his blood is not the blood, sweat and horror of American slavery. He does not have one drop of the blood of slavery in his body. His mother was a White woman and his father was an African man from Kenya. Unlike 99% of African Americans not one ancestor was an American, Caribbean or South American slave.

Slavery rests at the foundation of American capitalism and is often synonymous with the sugar, tobacco, and/or cotton plantations that fueled the Southern economy. What many may not know is that slavery also rests at the foundation of a great many notable corporations. From New York Life to Bank of America, to JPMorgan Chase to AIG to Wells Fargo, several American banking and insurance corporations have benefited from slavery. Many of these companies have acknowledged their involvement in slavery and offered apologies in an attempt to reconcile their tainted history but, is an apology enough?

History has consistently shown that slavery and segregation destroyed the *family life and the quality of life* for American slaves and our African

American descendants and simultaneously enhanced the quality of life for White Americans. From institutionalized racism to blocked social and economic opportunities, African Americans as a whole have been excluded from a way of life that all White Americans take for granted.

****

Apologies cannot compensate an entire people for all of the social and economic ills we faced as a result of our forefathers' enslavement. Apologies alone cannot address the residual effects of slavery and American segregation. Apologies cannot provide job opportunities to people who for over one hundred and fifty years have experienced high unemployment rates.

Had it not been for slave labor, many corporations would not be where they are today and for these companies to acknowledge their involvement in slavery and then simply say 'Oh, I'm sorry", is to downplay their role in and is little more than a futile attempt to correct a wrong by just an apology.

Instead of apologies, American Corporations could give back to the African American community by donating billions to Historically Black Universities and Colleges so that every African American child who wants a tuition free College scholarship can have one at a Black University.

And it's not just American corporations. Profits from the slave trade accumulated the huge amounts of money in the Western European banks and in the Western European insurance companies needed to finance not only the global shipping companies that put Europe and America at the head of highly lucrative world trade, but profits from slavery in the western hemisphere and profits from the Atlantic Slave Trade also financed both the scientific and industrial revolutions of the entire Western and American world.

****

Slavery and the theft of Africa made Western Europe and America great.

Slavery and the slaughter and wholesale extinction of most of the Native Americans and tribes were the water and fertilizer of the whole modern era and is the source of global Western Europe and American power, economically, technologically and militarily. The whole modern technological era was watered and fertilized with the bones and blood of hundreds and hundreds of millions of dead Africans and dead Indians. American Slavery was not just in the American south but lasted in the north until the 1840's.

Slave holders and the commodity crops of the South had a strong influence on United States politics and economy; New York City's economy was closely tied to the South through shipping and manufacturing, for instance. By 1822 half of its exports were related to cotton.

By 1810, 75 percent of all African Americans in the North were free. By 1840, virtually all African Americans in the North were free. Vermont's 1777 constitution made no allowance for slavery. In Massachusetts, slavery was successfully challenged in court in 1783 in a freedom suit by Quock Walker as being in contradiction to the state's new constitution of 1780 providing for equality of men. But freed slaves were highly subject to racial segregation, isolation, economic deprivation, social ostracism in the North, and it took decades for some states to extend the franchise to them.

Most northern states passed legislation for gradual abolition. As a result of this gradualist approach, New York did not free its last slaves until 1829, Rhode Island had five slaves still listed in the 1840 census, Pennsylvania's last slaves were freed in 1847, Connecticut did not completely abolish slavery until 1848, and slavery was not completely lifted in New Hampshire and New Jersey until the nationwide emancipation in 1865.

****

Many of the White Americans today who claimed their families arrived after slavery ended or were here during slavery, but had no real benefit from slavery are mistaken. There would be little to nothing in America, in terms of infrastructure for the later immigrations of White people to come over and add to it, if it were not for the slave labor from Africa and the later African American Slaves and descendants who built the two hundred and fifty years of White American privilege and entitlement.

Slave labor cleared away the huge forests, built the early ports and shipping docks for trade between the Americas and Western Europe. Slave labor loaded and unloaded the departing and arriving ships. In the American continents in general, both in North and South America, slave labor dug the canals for commerce. Slave labor drained the swamps to clear away the habitat of the swarms of mosquitoes. Dramatically reducing mosquitoes and swamps made greater White settlement across America possible because of the wide spread malaria carried by large swarms of mosquitoes from Virginia to Brazil. Blacks were used for this work because they were seen as more resistant to malaria than Whites and White diseases killed off the Indian slaves in droves.

Slave labor built the early roads and bridges in America. Slave labor laid down the cobblestones for Wall Street itself in New York City. Four centuries of slave trading and slave labor built up the United States and Western European banking system, so that these same banks and financial institutions could later make the loans needed to build the industries and manufacturing plants that slaves built and free Blacks could not get a job in.

Slaves were also artisans and craftsmen and not just farm laborers. On the large plantations Slaves were the iron workers, carpenters, brick layers and builders. Often these skilled African American Slaves were "rented out" for profit to other whites by the slave owners and did skilled non-farming work. We did not just plant, tend and harvest cotton, tobacco, rice and sugar cane.

****

Slavery was a source of wealth for many nations, and had been for centuries before the Western European and White American slave trading began. But the Western European and White American slave, segregation and racism system was especially evil, cruel, vile, and vicious.

It was based on hundreds of thousands of Western European and American White men with guns and cannons, killing, beating, raping, torturing, humiliating and degrading Black men and women. 99% percent of African slaves brought from Africa, were docile farmers, agriculturists and skilled craftsmen. Think of it as an alien race coming to America, destroying the military machine with superior weaponry and taking back to its planet only docile, White American water irrigators and farmers, because that's what they needed.

America and Western Europe didn't need Africa's warriors, they needed and took tens of millions of Africa's farmers and laborers, men, women and children and put them and their descendants into a worldwide slavery and bondage, inside and outside Africa. A Slavery that would last more than five hundred years, destroying the fabric of Africa, Africans, those of African descent and African Americans to this very day.

Our ancestors were worked, and worked and worked and worked and worked and worked and worked and worked to death, into early graves, for five hundred years building America's and Western Europe's trillions and trillions of dollars of intergenerational wealth. Africans and people of African descent and color all over the world, including African Americans in America got nothing in return.

Yet one of the first things I can remember hearing as a child is how I have to pull myself up by my own bootstraps, and I remember replying to that in a poem I wrote as a child by saying, *"But, Mr. Man, we ain't got no bootstraps to pull ourselves up by"*. Intergenerational poverty, year after year poverty, everyday poverty in the United States of America is a bitch. Just ask anybody in any poor black community, in any poor white community, in any city, in any town, in any village, in any housing project, in any ghetto in the United States of America, the so-called richest country on the face of the Earth, ever. Everyday poverty, until the day you die in poverty, is a bitch!!!

Never forget that the majority of the 14th century Western European common men and women were poverty stricken, disease ridden, malnourished, generally unwashed and horrifically nasty people who killed everything in their path and except for their ships and firearms, remained relatively technologically and economically backwards. That is, until the theft of Africa, India, the Americas and the five centuries of the Atlantic Slave Trade and White colonialism. The murder, raping and theft of Africa and most countries of color under colonialism made White Western Europe and America as rich and powerful as they are today.

CHAPTER 4

BLACK WALL STREET

Our Black communities in America have been under siege and oppressed since slavery ended and we began to form our own towns and communities in America. We have been under siege and attacked by White America for one hundred and fifty years as free people. A declaration of War by the White people of America has been waged against Black people in America for the two hundred and forty years of White American Independence from Great Britain.

Black Wall street was the name given to Greenwood Avenue, located in Tulsa, Oklahoma, where starting in 1910, this 35 square block area was both admired and envied by many individuals because the circulation of Black Dollars within the Black communities produced tremendously prosperous and wealthy groups of Black families and a vibrant black community. What made Black Wall street so powerful is that the Black dollar circulated anywhere from 36 to 1000 times, sometimes taking a whole year before the money left the community.

By 1921, the population of Black Wall Street had reached 11,000 and the community had its own bus line, thirteen churches, four hotels, tree drug stores, two high schools, two theaters, two newspapers, one hospital and a public library. In addition to that, they built nearly 200 two-and-three-story brick commercial buildings that housed professional offices for lawyers, doctors and dentists, clothing stores, grocery stores, nightclubs, restaurants and motels. Black Wall Street had become a strong commercial community.

African Americans had been subjected to segregationist policies during the early 1900's, therefore Black people were forced to live amongst each other, shop and spend money with one another. Investing African American dollars back in their own community, and servicing their community became the envy of America, produced a sense of accomplishment, pride and self-sufficiency.

One of the worst act of thousands of white racial violence acts in American history occurred on June 1, 1921, when Black Wall Street was burned to the ground by a mob of angry Whites after newspaper reporters wrongly claimed that a Black shoeshine boy had sexually assaulted a 17-year-old White girl in the lift of the office block where they both worked. A White lynch mob decided they would take matters in their own hands and tried to kill Rowland, which ultimately led to confrontation between the black and White communities and one of the most intentional genocides of Black people in American history.

The attack left more than 3,000 African Americans dead and nearly 600 African American successful businesses destroyed by fire.

CHAPTER 5

SLAVERY IN THE UNITED STATES OF AMERICA

If you the reader would like to know more about the foundation and progression of *The Atlantic Slave Trade*, a more in-depth account of slavery can be found in the book, *African American History In the United States of America - From Africa to President Barack Obama - An Anthology - Volume One* by Tony Rose (Amber Books) – www.amberbooks.com

WRITERS NOTE.

After having read *An Investigation and Study of The White People of America and Western Europe*, I think you'll agree with me that nothing much has changed. Overall, the Slave quarters, oops, I mean the ghetto is still under siege and the overseers, I mean, the police, are still killing and jailing us. The vast majority of the white population has no love or concern for African Americans, except as I said before, "for those who entertain them". White people still have all the political and enforcement power, because they are not afraid to lie, cheat, steal and murder, and the Dred Scott decision still holds true, "The Black man has no rights, which the White man is bound to respect".

So now I hope after all of this, you White people will know, "What's wrong with Black people". And it's in my very humble opinion, that the further "Study of the White People of America" and their hatred for Black People is badly needed.

CHAPTER 6

TARZAN AND JANE

AFRICA BEFORE THE TRANSATLANTIC SLAVE TRADE

Most educated, uneducated, rich or poor White Americans and White Western Europeans believe that Africa and Africans looked like a Tarzan and Jane movie starring Johnny Weismeller, before slavery, as well as, after slavery. My Grandfather Papa Ray always said that those White motherfuckers were the most ignorant people on the face of this Earth. He believed that totally, and hated White people and their racism, ignorance and stupidity, with a passion. During the Civil Rights Era of the 1960's my Grandmere' refused to call herself a black person, she would forever be a colored person or as she called herself "A Person of Color". My Papa Ray would have flown the Black Panther Party flag out the window and worn a dashiki if he thought that my Grandmere' wouldn't have thrown him out.

They were as funny as they could be, I would be a young teenager sitting with them in their Cambridge house on a Sunday, after church, and Papa Ray would be reading his Sunday newspaper with all the comics and everything and he would be raving up a storm about how he hated White people, how he was going to go to New York City to the Mosque and march with Malcolm X, and my Grandmere' would be ignoring him, while getting ready to go to her Eastern Star meeting that evening, while sipping on her Dewar's White Label Blended Scotch Whiskey and smoking her Parliament cigarettes.

****

The people and countries of West Africa and Africa had a rich and varied history and culture long before Western Europeans arrived.

Most White Americans and White Western Europeans think that Africa's history was not and is not important. They argued that Africans were inferior to Europeans and they used this to help justify slavery. However, the reality was very different. A study of African history shows that Africa was by no means inferior to Europe. The people who suffered the most from the Transatlantic Slave Trade were civilized, organized and technologically advanced people, long before the arrival of the White Western European countries, with their guns and cannons.

Egypt was the first of many great African cultures and civilizations. It lasted thousands of years and achieved many magnificent and incredible things in the fields of science, mathematics, medicine, technology and the arts. Egyptian civilization was already over 3000 years old by the time the city of Rome was just being built.

In West Africa, the kingdom of Ghana was a vast Empire that spread across an area the size of Western Europe. Between the ninth and thirteenth centuries, it traded in gold, salt and copper. It was like similar to a medieval European empire, with a collection of powerful local rulers, controlled by one king or emperor. Ghana was highly advanced and prosperous. It is said that the Ghanaian ruler had an army of 200,000 men.

The kingdoms of Benin and Ife were led by the Yoruba people and sprang up between the 11th and 12th centuries. The Ife civilization back as far as 500 B.C. and its people made objects from bronze, brass, copper, wood and ivory. Studies of the Benin show that they were highly skilled in ivory carving, pottery, rope and gum production.

From the thirteenth to the fifteenth century, the kingdom of Mali spread across much of West and North-East Africa. At its largest, the kingdom was 2000 kilometers wide and there was an organized trading system, with gold dust and agricultural produce being exported north. Mali reached its height in the 14th century. Cowrie shells were used as a form of currency and gold, salt and copper were traded.

Between, 1450-1550, the Songhay kingdom grew very powerful and prosperous. It had a well-organized system of government, a developed currency and it imported fabrics from Europe. Timbuktu became one of the most important places in the world. Libraries and universities were built and it became the meeting place for poets, scholars and artists from other parts of Africa and the Middle East.

****

The people and countries of West Africa and Africa had a rich and varied history and culture long before Western Europeans arrived. They had a wide variety of political arrangements including kingdoms, city-states and other organizations, each with their own languages and culture and we haven't even discussed Eastern or Southern African empires and civilizations.

The empire of Songhai and the kingdoms of Mali, Benin and Kongo were large and powerful with monarchs heading complex political structures governing hundreds of thousands of subjects. In other areas, political systems were smaller and weaker, relying on agreement between people at village level. As in 16th century war-torn Europe, the balance of power between political states and groups was constantly changing.

Art, learning and technology flourished and Africans were especially skilled in subjects like medicine, mathematics and astronomy and agriculture. As well as domestic goods, they made fine luxury items in bronze, ivory, gold and terracotta for both local use and trade.

Before the White Western Europeans came to West Africa with their guns and cannons, West Africans had traded with Western Europeans through merchants in North Africa for centuries. The first traders to sail down the West African coast were the Portuguese in the 15th century. Later the Dutch, British, French, English and Scandinavians followed. They were mainly interested in precious items such as gold, ivory and spices, particularly pepper.

In the 15th century White Western European traders, began bringing guns and cannons to Africa and began kidnapping and selling Africans as slaves in Europe. However, it was not until the 16th century, when White European and eventually White American plantation owners, in the "New World" wanted more and more slaves to satisfy the increasing demand for sugar in Europe, that The Transatlantic Slave Trade became the dominant trade, and destroyed West Africa, Africa, Africans, African Americans and everyone of African descent to this very day.

CHAPTER 6

BLACK LIVES MATTER

THE KILLING OF BLACK MEN, WOMEN AND
CHILDREN IN AMERICA

THE POLICE KILLED MORE THAN 100 UNARMED AFRICAN
AMERICAN MEN, WOMEN AND
CHILDREN IN 2015.

"The White Man" police killings of unarmed African Americans has nothing to do with more police sensitivity training, it has to do with the subliminal hate "The White Man" has for African Americans in America. That's why they can shoot down and kill an African American twelve-year-old child, like Tamir Rice, in seconds.

Since 1800 tens and tens of thousands of African American men, women and children have been killed and that's outside of the tens of millions killed, lynched and burned alive, drawn and quartered during slavery.

These African American men, women and children have been shot down and killed by white policemen for nothing, just crimes supposed, and without the benefit of doubt by "White Men".

In just two years, 2014 and 2015, more unarmed African men, women and children were killed in the United States of America, then any terrorist attack in the last ten years.

1. **Keith Childress, 12/31/15**

Las Vegas, NV: The U.S. Marshals were conducting surveillance on the man and requested help from Metro when he fled. When police caught up with him, they claimed he had an "unknown object" in his hand. Assuming it was a gun, they shot him dead. The object turned out to be a cellphone. No officers were charged with a crime for killing Keith.

****

2. **Bettie Jones, 12/25/15**

Chicago, IL: Chicago police shot Bettie Jones in the neck "accidentally" while trying to help a neighbor deal with a domestic disturbance involving his son, Quintonio Legrier. The neighbor said he called police when his son tried to break his door down early in the morning, and that Jones was shot when she opened the door to direct officers when they arrived. No officers have been charged with a crime for killing Bettie.

****

3. **Kevin Matthews, 12/23/15**

Dearborn, MI: An officer pursued Matthews, who was reportedly wanted on a misdemeanor warrant, authorities said. The officer attempted to subdue Matthews with pepper spray and shot him during a struggle when Matthews reached for his gun, police said. Family members identified Matthews after the shooting and said he was being treated for schizophrenia. No officers have been charged with a crime for killing Kevin.

4. **Leroy Browning, 12/20/15**

Palmdale, CA: Deputies say Browning, 30, fled when they were attempting to arrest him for a DUI. They claim he put deputies in a "bear hug" and reached for a firearm before being shot by deputies. No officers have been charged with a crime for killing Leroy.

****

5. **Roy Nelson, 12/19/15**

Hayward, CA: Hayward police responded to a report of a man needing an emergency mental health evaluation. After arriving, officers determined Roy needed an involuntary psychiatric hold and put him in the back of a police car. On the way to the hospital, police say Roy tried to kick out the car's rear window. The police forced Roy into a leg restraint, after which Roy died. No officers have been charged with a crime for killing Roy.

****

6. **Miguel Espinal, 12/8/15**

Yonkers, NY: Miguel Espinal, 36, was shot and killed by NYPD officers in an incident that started with a traffic stop in the Bronx. Espinal fled the stop, prompting a police chase that ended in a wrong-way crash.

After the crash, Espinal left the vehicle and ran to the surrounding Tibbetts Brook Park, where police killed him.

Espinal's family said he ran from officers because he doesn't have a license. "Whether he ran from the cops or not, it doesn't justify that he got shot. It doesn't justify that," Justin Juble, Espinal's brother, said. No officers have been charged with a crime for killing Miguel.

****

7. Nathaniel Pickett, 11/19/15

Barstow, CA: Nathaniel, 29, allegedly jumped a fence and "became unco-operative" when a deputy stopped to question him, police said. When the deputy tried to handcuff Pickett, they claim a fight broke out ending when the deputy shot Nathaniel. No officers have been charged with a crime for killing Nathaniel.

****

8. Tiara Thomas, 11/18/15

Portage, IN: A Hammond police officer killed Tiara, who was the mother of three of his children. The motive is suspected to be financial. Officer Kevin Campbell was charged with murder for killing Tiara.

****

9. Cornelius Brown, 11/18/15

Opa-locka, FL: Police said they shot and killed Brown after he hit the windshield of a patrol car and ignored commands from police. He was unarmed. No officers have been charged with a crime for killing Cornelius.

****

10. Chandra Weaver, 11/17/15

Kansas City, MO: Chandra, 48, was killed by Kansas City, MO police, who crashed their patrol car into the driver's side of her Pontiac Grand Am. No officers have been charged with a crime for killing Chandra.

****

11. Jamar Clark, 11/15/15

Minneapolis, MN: Two Minneapolis police officers shot Clark, claiming he "interfered" with emergency responders helping an assault victim. Activists and witnesses maintain that Clark was unarmed and handcuffed when he was shot.

No officers have been charged with a crime for killing Jamar.

****

12. Richard Perkins, 11/15/15

Oakland, CA: Oakland police were towing vehicles near 90th Ave. and Bancroft Ave. when they claim Richard, 39, approached them and "pointed a firearm in their direction." They shot Richard multiple times. Police later revealed Richard's "firearm" was actually a toy gun. No officers have been charged with a crime for killing Richard.

****

13. **Stephen Tooson, 11/12/15**

Birmingham, AL: An officer crashed into Stephen's SUV while rushing to respond to a domestic call, killing him. He was 45 years old. No officers have been charged with a crime for killing Stephen.

****

14. **Michael Lee Marshall, 11/11/15**

Denver, CO: Michael, a 50-year-old mentally ill man, apparently posed no physical threat when three sheriff's deputies restrained him into unconsciousness at the Denver jail. He died after nine days on life support.

No officers have been charged with a crime for killing Michael.

****

15. **Alonzo Smith, 11/1/15**

Washington, DC: Alonzo Smith, 27, died while handcuffed in the custody of DC special police officers. Special police officers are armed security guards licensed by the city. No officers have been charged with a crime for killing Alonzo.

****

16. Yvens Seide, 10/31/15

Big Cypress, FL: Officer Gary Paul Evelyn struck Seide, 33, with a marked Seminole police pick-up truck. Seide was hit with the truck's left front, according to the Florida Highway Patrol. No officers have been charged with a crime for killing Yvens.

****

17. Anthony Ashford, 10/27/15

San Diego, CA: A San Diego Harbor officer claimed he confronted Ashford, 29, after seeing him "looking into cars" near Nimitz Boulevard. After being tased, police claim Ashford reached for the officer's gun before being shot and killed. No officers have been charged with a crime for killing Anthony.

****

18. Lamontez Jones, 10/20/15

San Diego, CA: Police say Lamontez, 39, was "causing a disturbance" downtown and ran when police approached him. Police shot Lamontez multiple times, claiming he aimed a gun at them. Police later revealed that the gun was a toy.

No officers have been charged with a crime for killing Lamontez.

****

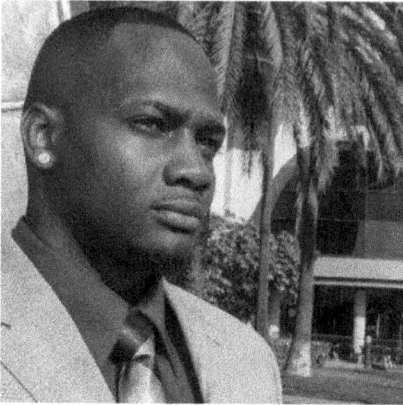

19. **Rayshaun Cole, 10/17/15**

Chula Vista, CA: A U.S. Customs and Border Protection officer shot and killed her boyfriend Rayshaun, 30, in their Chula Vista apartment, telling police that she was defending herself and he had hit her. No officers have been charged with a crime for killing Rayshaun.

****

20. **Paterson Brown, 10/17/15**

Richmond, VA: An off-duty police officer shot and killed Brown, 18, claiming he got into the officer's car at a gas station and began driving it while the officer was waiting for it to be washed. A witness told reporters that the officer identified himself as a police officer and ordered Brown to get out of the car. The officer claims Brown "made a sudden movement", before the officer shot him. No officers have been charged with a crime for killing Paterson.

****

21. **Christopher Kimble, 10/3/15**

East Cleveland, OH: Christopher, 22, was struck and killed by a police cruiser while crossing the street. The cruiser was speeding on its way to a reported car crash. No officers have been charged with a crime for killing Christopher.

****

22. **Junior Prosper, 9/28/15**

North Miami, FL: Junior Prosper crashed the car he was driving, a cab, on the highway and allegedly began to run away. An officer chased Junior, claiming Junior bit his finger before the officer shot and killed him. Prosper's mother, Marie, said the police were not telling the truth about him. "He's very nice, he's a person who respects all types of people. He's not aggressive. Whoever said that is lying." He leaves behind three children, and his wife is expecting a fourth. No officers have been charged with a crime for killing Junior.

****

23. **Keith McLeod, 9/23/15**

Reisterstown, MD: An employee at a pharmacy called police to report that Mc-Leod had tried to use a fake prescription. The responding officer spotted McLeod in a parking lot near the pharmacy and fatally shot him after claiming he reached "around to the small of his back and abruptly [whipped] his hand around and [pointed] it toward the officer, as if with a weapon," according to police. He 19 years old and unarmed. No officers have been charged with a crime for killing Keith.

****

24. **Wayne Wheeler, 9/7/15**

Lathrop, MI: A Lathrop police officer was grilling in his backyard when Wayne, his 44-year-old neighbor, allegedly jumped the fence. The officer fought Wayne and struck him in the head, knocking him down. Wayne was pronounced dead at the scene by a medic. No officers have been charged with a crime for killing Wayne.

113

****

25. India Kager, 9/5/15

Virginia Beach, VA: Navy Veteran India Kager was in a vehicle with her 4 month-old baby and Angelo Perry, who was being followed by unmarked police vehicles. When India parked at a 7-Eleven, the officers also parked and approached the car. Officers claim Angelo shot at them before they shot over thirty times at the vehicle. Angelo and India were killed, while the baby was unharmed. Kager's mother disputes the police narrative. "It was very clear to me that India was not part of the police investigation based on the responses I got from police. She had nothing to do with it. She was totally innocent," she told the Washington Post. "Did they find any weapons on India? Did she pose a threat? Why did [police] shoot into a car with a baby and woman who had nothing to do with their investigation? I'm devastated because she should still be alive nursing her son, my grandson," she explained. "We're talking about a very beautiful soul that should still be here. She was unarmed, she was completely innocent. They shot indiscriminately." No officers have been charged with a crime for killing India.

****

26. Tyree Crawford, 9/1/15

Newark, NJ: Officers responded to a carjacking involving juvenile suspects. When the vehicle was pulled over and passengers got out of vehicle, Crawford was hit by the front end of an oncoming police vehicle, killing him. No officers have been charged with a crime for killing Tyree.

****

27. **James Carney III, 8/31/15**

Cincinnati, OH: Police claim they saw James, 48, assaulting a woman in a car at an ATM. They tased James twice, causing him to die from his injuries. No officers have been charged with a crime for killing James.

****

28. **Felix Kumi, 8/28/15**

New York, NY: Kumi, 61, was an innocent bystander during a sting operation. He was shot by an undercover NYPD officer while allegedly standing near a suspect. No officers have been charged with a crime for killing Felix.

****

29. **Wendell Hall, 8/27/15**

Kansas City, KS: Wendell Hall, 50, was a passenger in a vehicle that was struck by a police car. He was killed immediately. No officers have been charged with a crime for killing Wendell.

Dec 28, 2015 2 DeRay McKesson

****

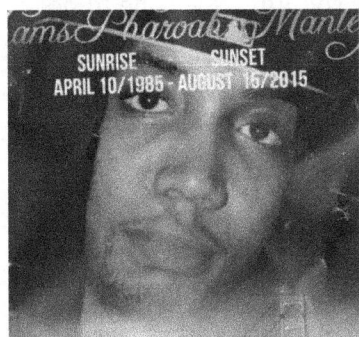

30. **Asshams Manley, 8/14/15**

Spauldings, MD: Officer saw Manley, 30, fleeing a car crash. The officer chased Manley and shot him, claiming Manley reached for his gun. A second officer arrived and stunned Manley with a Taser, then a third officer arrived forcibly restrained him. Manley died soon after. No officers have been charged with a crime for killing Asshams.

115

****

31. Christian Taylor, 8/7/15

Arlington, TX: Christian, 19, entered a car dealership after hours and can be seen in security surveillance footage jumping on cars and smashing the windows of several vehicles. Six Arlington police arrived and Brad Miller, a rookie cop, fatally shot unarmed Christian. Has since been fired from his station. No officers have been charged with a crime for killing Christian.

****

32. Troy Robinson, 8/6/15

Decatur, GA:

Police claim Troy, 32, ran from an officer after a traffic stop. The officer deployed his Taser, causing Robinson to fall from an eight-foot wall, sustaining fatal injuries. No officers have been charged with a crime for killing Troy.

****

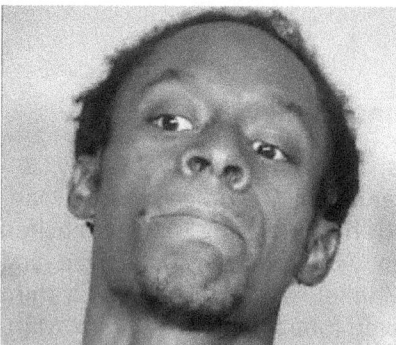

33. Brian Day, 7/25/15

Las Vegas, NV: After speaking to police who were investigating a beating of one of his neighbors, police claim Day went into his apartment and returned with a toy gun. Two officers shot and fatally wounded him after he attempted to "shoot" them with the toy gun.

No officers have been charged with a crime for killing Brian.

****

34. Michael Sabbie, 7/22/15

Texarkana, TX: Police sprayed Michael Sabbie with a chemical agent while in jail, causing him to become unresponsive and die soon afterwards.

No officers have been charged with a crime for killing Michael.

****

35. Billy Ray Davis, 7/20/15

Houston, TX: A police officer claims Davis threatened him. The officer reportedly called for backup, they restrained him and called paramedics. Davis became unconscious and died while being transported to the hospital. No officers have been charged with a crime for killing Billy.

****

36. Samuel DuBose, 7/19/15

Cincinnati, OH: Police initially said that an officer pulled DuBose over for a routine traffic stop which escalated into some type of altercation, and that DuBose dragged an officer with his vehicle for a distance before the officer fired. That account was later disproven by body camera footage released by Cincinnati prosecutor Joseph Deters. University of Cincinnati Officer Ray Tensing has been charged with murder for killing Samuel.

****

37. Darrius Stewart, 7/17/15

Memphis, TN: Stewart was stopped by police for a broken headlight. Authorities said he was placed in the back of a patrol car, unhandcuffed, while officers ran his name. When the officers returned to hand-cuff Stewart and take him into custody for outstanding warrants, police said he became "combative" and struck an officer with the handcuffs. The officer then drew his gun and fired. Stewart's mother told local news that her son had never been arrested and that the warrants were for someone else with the same name. No officers have been charged with a crime for killing Darrius.

****

38. Albert Davis, 7/17/15

Orlando, FL: Albert Davis, 23, was shot and killed by an Orlando police officer who had been called after reports of a fight in the area involving five men. The officer deployed his Taser and then fired his gun, after an alleged 'struggle' with Davis. Despite police saying Davis was 'very, very violent' towards the officer, the officer did not sustain any injuries. No officers have been charged with a crime for killing Albert.

****

39. Sandra Bland, 7/13/15

Waller County, TX: Sandra Bland, 28, was pulled over for a routine traffic stop, which the deputy quickly escalated by removing Sandra from the vehicle and physically restraining her. She would later die in a jail cell under dubious circumstances. Trooper Brian Encina was charged with perjury for lying about the events leading up to Sandra's arrest.

****

40. **Salvado Ellswood, 7/12/15**

Plantation, FL: Police claim that 36-year-old Ellswood, who was released from prison less than a month earlier and was homeless, struck an officer and shook off a Taser before being fatally shot. No officers have been charged with a crime for killing Salvado.

****

41. **George Mann, 7/11/15**

Stonewall, GA: Police were called to a Stone Mountain home after a caller said Mann was irate and locked in a garage. Officers claim they attempted to negotiate with Mann before tasing him. The 35-year-old became unresponsive and pronounced dead at a nearby hospital. No officers have been charged with a crime for killing George.

****

42. **Jonathan Sanders, 7/8/15**

Stonewall, MS: Jonathan, 39, was in a buggy pulled by horses in Stonewall when Officer Kevin Herrington pulled up behind him. The lights apparently scared the horses and Sanders was trying to calm them when Herrington choked Sanders with a flashlight. No officers have been charged with a crime for killing Jonathan.

****

43. **Victor Larosa III, 7/2/15**

Jacksonville, FL: Victor Larosa was shot after tripping and falling to the ground while fleeing officers following an undercover sting operation against drug deals, according to the sheriff's office. The officer alleged that he opened fire because Larosa reached into his waistband. No weapon was recovered from the scene. No officers have been charged with a crime for killing Victor.

****

44. **Kevin Judson, 7/1/15**

McMinnville, OR: Kevin Judson, 24, was shot and killed by a deputy following a traffic stop, after Judson allegedly tried to flee in the deputy's patrol car. No officers have been charged with a crime for killing Kevin.

****

45. **Spencer McCain, 6/25/15**

Owings Mills, MD: Police responding to a domestic call early Thursday entered a condominium after hearing arguing inside and fatally shot McCain, claiming they believed he had a gun. McCain was later revealed to be unarmed and died at a nearby hospital. No officers have been charged with a crime for killing Spencer.

****

46. **Kevin Bajoie, 6/20/15**

Baton Rouge, LA: Police responding to calls of two men fighting tased 31-year-old unarmed Bajoie after they claim he "tried to attack officers". Bajoie later died at a nearby hospital. No officers have been charged with a crime for killing Kevin.

****

47. **Zamiel Crawford, 6/20/15**

McAllah, AL: Crawford, 21, was chased by Leeds police and Jefferson County sheriff's deputies, ending when his vehicle rammed a deputy's vehicle. He was unarmed and police tased him, but police have yet to say exactly what killed him. No officers have been charged with a crime for killing Zamiel.

****

48. **Jermaine Benjamin, 6/16/15**

Vero Beach, FL: Deputies responding to a disturbance call claim they found Benjamin, 42, acting erratic. A deputy subdued Benjamin by putting his knee into the back of Benjamin's neck and keeping his face pressed against the ground. "By the time they turned him back over, he was gone," Benjamin's cousin, Lateesia Jordan, told WPBF 25 News. No officers have been charged with a crime for killing Jermaine.

****

49. **Kris Jackson, 6/15/15**

South Lake Tahoe, CA: An officer responding to a domestic disturbance fatally shot Jackson, claiming to see the 22-year-old man climb through a back window at a Lake Tahoe motel.

Jackson's family questions whether the officer fol-

121

lowed proper protocol. Jackson's girlfriend, who was at the scene, did not hear a command to stop from the officer. She also questions whether Jackson was a threat. "He was shot while climbing out a window," Laskin wrote. "Does that sound like he posed a threat?" No officers have been charged with a crime for killing Kris.

****

50. Alan Craig Williams, 6/13/15

Greenville, SC: Alan Craig Williams was driving on Poinsett Highway when a Greenville County deputy struck his moped from behind, killing him in the crash. No officers have been charged with a crime for killing Alan.

****

51. Ross Anthony, 6/9/15

Dallas, TX: Police claim Ross Anthony was banging his fists on the hood of an ambulance and got into another person's vehicle when they arrived. Officers claim they attempted to talk Anthony out of the car, choosing to reach in and grab him when he opened the door. When he allegedly resisted, the officer tased Anthony, which ended up killing him. No officers have been charged with a crime for killing Ross.

****

52. Richard Gregory Davis, 5/31/15

Rochester, NY: Davis drove into a truck and a church before leaving his vehicle. Police and firefighters confronted Davis, who returned to his vehicle and locked himself inside. He then left his vehicle and ran at responders. Officer Thomas Frye shot him with a stun gun, causing him to die soon afterwards. No officers have been charged with a crime for killing Richard

53. **Markus Clark, 5/21/15**

Fort Lauderdale, FL: Deputies were called to a robbery at an Exxon gas station on Northwest 27th Avenue. When they arrived, deputies found Clark struggling with one of the clerks. Deputies fought Clark. Clark was brought to the hospital before he died. No officers have been charged with a crime for killing Markus.

****

54. **Lorenzo Hayes, 5/13/15**

Spokane, WA: While enroute to jail, police said Lorenzo began kicking on the back of the patrol car. Jail staff took him into the booking area while he was handcuffed. Lorenzo died soon afterwards, while jail staff prepared to place him in a restraint chair. No officers have been charged with a crime for killing Lorenzo.

****

55. **De'Angelo Stallworth, 5/12/15**

Jacksonville, FL: Two Jacksonville police officers fatally shot Stallworth at a Westside apartment complex. Stallworth allegedly pointed a gun at an officer, then dropped the gun and ran away. Officers shot him as he was running unarmed, claiming they thought he still had a gun and he turned and faced them. No officers have been charged with a crime for killing De'Angelo.

56. Dajuan Graham, 5/12/15

Silver Spring, MD: Police respond to a disturbance call about a man on the street acting erratically. When police approached Graham, they claim he continued to stand in the middle of the street with his hands in his pockets. According to police, officers asked Graham four times to remove his hands from his pockets, but he "refused to comply" and "assumed a threatening stance." Police tased Graham in the stomach and right, upper thigh, then arrested him. After Graham arrived at the hospital, police removed his handcuffs and once again restrained him after he allegedly assaulted an officer and security guard. Graham died a few days later. No officers have been charged with a crime for killing Dajuan.

****

57. Brandon Glenn, 5/6/15

Los Angeles, CA: Glenn was allegedly panhandling outside a bar in Venice when a customer complained that he was harassing customers. He wound up in a scuffle with a bouncer and two officers, one of whom shot and killed him. After viewing unreleased tape of the incident, LAPD police chief Charlie Beck said: 'Any time an unarmed person is shot by a Los Angeles police officer, it takes extraordinary circumstances to justify that. I have not seen those extraordinary circumstances. No officers have been charged with a crime for killing Brandon.

****

58. Reginald Moore, 5/6/15

Greenville, MS:

Greenville Police Sergeant Kvonya Moore shot and killed her husband Reginald Moore. Moore and her husband had just returned home from her birthday party when the shooting occurred, and the couple's two children were at home when it happened. Reginald Moore had been shot in the head and died at Delta Regional Medical Center. Moore, who oversees Washington County's CrimeStoppers Program was suspended with pay pending action by the Greenville City Council. Sgt. Kvonya Moore was charged with murder for killing Reginald.

59. **Nuwnah Laroche, 5/6/15**

Ridgefield Park, NJ: State police officers engaged in a high speed pursuit crashed and killed two pedestrians, Jason and Nuwnah. No officers have been charged with a crime for killing Nuwnah.

****

60. **Jason Champion, 5/6/15**

Ridgefield Park, NJ: State police officers engaged in a high speed pursuit crashed and killed two pedestrians, Jason and Nuwnah. No officers have been charged with a crime for killing Jason.

****

61. **Bryan Overstreet, 4/28/15**

Sylvester, GA: 30-year old Bryan Overstreet was run over by a Worth County deputy in the middle of the street. No officers have been charged with a crime for killing Bryan.

125

62. **Terrance Kellom, 4/27/15**

Detroit, MI: A fugitive task force involving ICE and officers with the Detroit Police Department — was attempting to serve a warrant at the home. Kellom, 20, was shot and killed after an officer "felt threatened." No officers have been charged with a crime for killing Terrance.

****

63. **David Felix, 4/25/15**

New York, NY: David, who was a schizophrenic living in a home for the mentally ill, was said by police to have "involved them in a struggle", in which officers shot him to death. No officers have been charged with a crime for killing Terrance.

****

64. **Lashonda Ruth Belk, 4/24/15**

West End, NC: Local police chased a 25-year-old suspect after he fled a traffic stop, causing him to lose control of his car and crash into a tree, killing passengers Lashonda Ruth Belk and Gregory Daquan Harris. No officers were charged with a crime for killing Lashonda.

****

65. **Gregory Daquan Harris, 4/24/15**

West End, NC: Local police chased a 25-year-old suspect after he fled a traffic stop, causing him to lose control of his car and crash into a tree, killing passengers Lashonda Ruth Belk and Gregory Daquan Harris. No officers were charged with a crime for killing Gregory.

126

****

66. **Terry Lee Chatman, 4/23/15**

Houston, TX: Terry was struck by a Houston police vehicle while on a bicycle heading southbound on MLK. The impact killed Chatman. No officers have been charged with a crime for killing Terry.

****

67. **William Chapman, 4/22/15**

Portsmouth, VA: A Walmart security called the police about a shoplifter. Police found William in the parking lot. Officer Stephen Rankin pulled his taser out, and claims the taser got knocked out of his hand during a "tussle". The policeman pulled out his gun and claims William took off his shirt as though he was ready to fight. The officer opened fire, killing William. Officer Stephen Rankin was charged with murder for killing William.

****

68. **Samuel Harrell, 4/21/15**

Beacon, NY: Samuel Harrell, 30, was involved in a confrontation with corrections officers at the Fishkill Correctional Facility, during which up to 20 officers repeatedly punched and kicked him while he was handcuffed on the ground, according to a New York Times report. The Orange County medical examiner ruled Harrell's cause of death as homicide 'following physical altercation with corrections officers'. No officers have been charged with a crime for killing Samuel.

****

69. **Freddie Gray, 4/19/15**

Baltimore, MD: Freddie Gray died from injuries sustained during a prolonged ride in a police van while handcuffed and shackled on the floor. He was arrested after catching the eye of a police officer and running away.

Six officers have been charged with crimes including murder for killing Freddie.

****

70. **Norman Cooper, 4/19/15**

San Antonio, TX: Police were called on a report of a family disturbance and found the subject under the influence of "some sort of narcotic." Police claim Norman was "uncooperative" and wouldn't be escorted out so police fired a Taser at him. Police claim Norman pulled the probes of the Taser out and a second Taser was fired at him. Shortly after, Norman became unresponsive and was pronounced dead at the scene. No officers have been charged with a crime for killing Norman.

****

71. **Brian Acton, 4/18/15**

Columbia, TN: Brian Acton was reportedly naked, drunk, and attempting to assault an acquaintance when police captured him, subdued and handcuffed him. He stopped breathing shortly thereafter. No officers have been charged with a crime for killing Brian.

****

128

72. **Darrell Brown, 4/17/15**

Hagerstown, MD: Police responded to a call of a man attempting to break-into a house. Police claim Darrell made an "aggressive stance" toward them and tased him an unknown number of times. He became unresponsive and was put in an ambulance and died at the hospital early the next morning. No officers have been charged with a crime for killing Darrell.

****

73. **Frank Shephard III, 4/15/15**

Houston, TX: Police tried to initiate a traffic stop due to "suspicious activity." Frank, 41, got out of the vehicle and then appeared to reach back into the vehicle when the two officers fired on him and killed him. No weapon was found in the vehicle. No officers have been charged with a crime for killing Frank.

****

74. **Walter Scott, 4/4/15**

North Charleston, SC: Scott was pulled over by North Charleston police officer Michael Slager for a minor traffic violation. Scott fled but Slager caught up with him and attempted to deploy his Taser. The Taser was not effective and as Scott ran away, Slager opened fire. The final altercation was caught on video. Officer Slager has been charged with murder for killing Walter.

75. Donald "Dontay" Ivy, 4/2/15

Albany, NY: Officers questioned Ivy, a paranoid schizophrenic with a heart condition. He fled down Second Street. Officers chased Ivy, shooting him with a Taser at least once. The Taser failed to subdue Ivy, whom they chased and handcuffed. When he stopped breathing, officers attempted CPR and called for help. Ivy died at Albany Medical Center. No officers have been charged with a crime for killing Donald.

****

76. Eric Harris, 4/2/15

Tulsa, OK: Harris fled an arrest after he sold a gun to undercover officers working a sting operation. He was caught by officers and shot by a 73-year-old part-time reserve deputy, who said he intended to use a Taser. Harris told officers 'I'm losing my breath,' to which one replied: 'Fuck your breath. Deputy Bates was charged with manslaughter for killing Eric.

****

77. Phillip White, 3/31/15

Vineland, NJ: White became unconscious as police attempted to take him into custody after reports that he was screaming. Officers allege White tried to grab the arresting officer's gun. Video shows White, clearly dazed, flailing on the ground as an officer strikes him and orders a police dog to attack. The hacker group Anonymous threatened the Vineland Police Department over the incident. No officers have been charged with a crime for killing Phillip.

78. **Dominick Wise, 3/30/15**

Culpeper, VA: An officer saw Dominick Wise, 30, "acting erratically by walking in circles in the middle of the street." The officer chased and confronted Wise and tased him an undetermined amount of times, killing him. No officers have been charged with a crime for killing Dominick.

＊＊＊＊

79. **Jason Moland, 3/29/15**

Ceres, CA: An off-duty police officer and a woman were in a park at night, and Moland approached them. There was a confrontation in which Moland pointed a BB gun, and the off-duty police officer shot Moland to death. No officers have been charged with a crime for killing Jason.

＊＊＊＊

80. **Nicholas Thomas, 3/24/15**

Atlanta, GA: Nicholas, a mechanic, was at his job when police called his boss and told them they were going to serve a warrant on the suspect. When police arrived Nicholas started driving the car he was working on around the business. Police opened fire and killed him. No officers have been charged with a crime for killing Nicholas.

81. Denzel Brown, 3/22/15

Bayshore, NY: Denzel Brown, 21, was suspected of shoplifting from a Best Buy. Police responded and found him hiding in the parking lot. Denzel attempted to open car doors in lot. Police claim he tried to steal a car from a couple with children in back seat. Officers shot and killed him. No officers were charged with a crime for killing Denzel.

****

82. Brandon Jones, 3/19/15

Cleveland, OH: Officers reported that they responded to a robbery call at Parkwood Grocery early in the morning when the store was closed. Accounts vary about the time of the shooting. Officers say they had a scuffle with Jones, who had a bag, and they shot him to death. There was no weapon found on Jones. No officers were charged with a crime for killing Brandon.

****

83. Askari Roberts, 3/17/15

Rome, GA: Roberts, 35, was showing signs of paranoia and thought a gang was coming to kill him. His wife pried his hands away from his son and police arrived and Tased him two or three times until he became unresponsive and died at the hospital. No officers have been charged with a crime for killing Askari.

84. Terrance Moxley, 3/10/15

Mansfield, OH: Police say Terrance was displaying "violent behavior" at a community service location. Police tasered him, he broke free and they tasered him again. He went into medical distress and died at the hospital. No officers have been charged with a crime for killing Terrance.

****

85. Anthony Hill, 3/9/15

Chamblee, GA: Police were responding to complaints about a naked man knocking on doors in an apartment complex. A deputy said Hill ran at him several times and ignored demands to stop. No officers have been charged with a crime for killing Anthony.

****

86. Bernard Moore, 3/6/15

Atlanta, GA: Moore was crossing a highway to get to the store where he worked when he was struck by a police car. Surveillance footage from a gas station showed the police car did not have its lights or siren on. Moore's family have accused the officer of speeding. The officer was charged with misdemeanor vehicular homicide.

87. **Naeschylus Vinzant, 3/6/15**

Aurora, CO: Officers say Vincent was wanted for violating parole. A SWAT team officer attempted to arrest him, ending up shooting him to death, claiming he didn't realize Naeschylus was unarmed. No officers have been charged with a crime for killing Naeschylus.

****

88. **Tony Robinson, 3/6/15**

Madison, WI: Police claim unarmed Tony Robinson attacked an officer who responded to calls for help from friends and nearby residents over his "erratic and aggressive behavior". The officer shot him seven times. Robinson's family filed a federal civil rights lawsuit against the officer and the city on August 12. No officers have been charged with a crime for killing Tony.

****

89. **Charly Leundeu "Africa" Keunang, 3/1/15**

Los Angeles, CA: 4 - 5 police officers are seen on video surrounding Africa on the ground and wrestling with him. Whether or not he actually reached for an officer's gun is unclear, but there are at least five gunshots heard on the video. No officers have been charged with a crime for killing Africa.

90. Darrell Gatewood, 3/1/15

Oklahoma City, OK: Police responded to a disturbance call about a man breaking things and "fighting with the air." When they arrived at the scene, Darrell started fighting with them. Deputies tased Darrell an unknown number of times and he went into cardiac arrest and was pronounced dead at the hospital. No officers have been charged with a crime for killing Darrell.

****

91. Deontre Dorsey, 3/1/15

White Plains, MD: Deontre Dorsey lost control of his car, coming to rest against a tree in a median. Witnesses called 911 saying Dorsey was "flopping like a fish." After Dorsey, who was having a seizure, rolled on his stomach and reached for a firefighter's leg, police ordered him to put his hands behind his back. When Dorsey failed to comply and tried to stand up, police tasered him in the back several times. Dorsey was later handcuffed and placed in leg shackles at the scene and stopped moving or breathing. He was a father of four. No officers have been charged with a crime for killing Deontre.

****

92. Thomas Allen Jr., 2/28/15

Wellston, MO: An officer pulled over a vehicle driven by Thomas Allen for a traffic violation. While questioning Thomas, a passenger got into the car and attempted to drive away. The officer fatally shot Thomas who died in the hospital the next day. No officers have been charged with a crime for killing Thomas.

135

93. Calvon Reid, 2/22/15

Coconut Creek, FL: Police said they found Reid injured and in an 'agitated, combative state' in a gated retirement community. He was tasered at least three times and went into cardiac arrest, according to lawyers. Authorities did not disclose the death until witness accounts were published by the media. Coconut Bay's police chief promptly retired. Medical examiners ruled the death a homicide by electrocution. No officers have been charged with a crime for killing Calvon.

****

94. Terry Price, 2/20/15

Tulsa, OK: Deputies responded to a call from casino security saying the subject who was banned from the premises was there and needed to be removed. The subject fled the scene and then returned. He ran into the woods where police tasered him. The subject collapsed and died. No officers have been charged with a crime for killing Terry.

****

95. Natasha McKenna, 2/8/15

Fairfax, VA: Police used a stun gun on McKenna, who had schizophrenia, claiming she "refused to comply" with deputies' commands and "physically resisted" them as they prepared her for transport to Alexandria to face charges there, the sheriff's office said. No officers have been charged with a crime for killing Natasha.

96. **Jeremy Lett, 2/4/15**

Tallahassee, FL: An officer responding to a burglary call at an apartment complex encountered Lett, and the two entered into a physical confrontation. The officer claims to have tried the Taser, but in the rain he only shocked himself. The officer claims Lett had the officer pinned to the ground when the officer shot and killed him.

No officers have been charged with a crime for killing Jeremy.

****

97. **Alvin Haynes, 1/26/15**

San Bruno, CA: Alvin, an inmate, died after deputies attempted to search him at San Francisco County Jail No. 5 in San Bruno. Deputies claim he had an envelope in his hand that the deputies were trying to examine and "a confrontation ensued". No officers have been charged with a crime for killing Alvin.

****

98. **Tiano Meton, 1/22/15**

Sierra Blanca, TX: Meton drove through a West Texas checkpoint without stopping and drove 30 more miles before he stopped. "Four agents approached the vehicle and one of them yelled 'gun,'" the AP reported. Two of the agents fired their weapons at the vehicle. A toy gun was found in Meton's vehicle. No officers have been charged with a crime for killing Tiano.

****

99. **Andre Larone Murphy Sr., 1/7/15**

Norfolk, NE: An officer responding to a disturbance call at a Super 8 Motel struggled with Murphy, using a taser against him. Murphy died soon after at Faith Regional Health Services in Norfolk, NE. No officers have been charged with a crime for killing Andre.

****

100. **Brian Pickett, 1/6/15**

Los Angeles, CA: Pickett's mother called police to report he was under the influence and had threatened her. When police arrived, Pickett allegedly charged at them and was tased by a deputy. He stopped breathing when the paramedics arrived and was pronounced dead at an area hospital. No officers have been charged with a crime for killing Brian.

****

101. **Leslie Sapp, 1/6/15**

Knoxville, PA: Marshals went to serve a warrant on Leslie. They shot and killed Leslie, claiming he pointed a toy gun at them. No officers have been charged with a crime for killing Leslie.

****

102. **Matthew Ajibade, 1/1/15**

Savannah, GA: Ojibade's girlfriend called 911 to ask police to take him to the hospital because he was having a manic episode (he had bipolar disorder). Instead, they arrested him and took him to the Chatham County Detention Center. The Sheriff's Office claims that he fought officers, so they put him in a restraining chair. He died in the restraining chair. Deputy Kenny was convicted of cruelty to an inmate and Deputy Evans was convicted of public records fraud and three counts of perjury for killing Matthew.

138

ABOUT THE AUTHOR

Tony Rose, Publisher/CEO, Amber Communications Group, Inc.
2013 NAACP Image Award Winner for Outstanding Literature.
2014 African American Publisher of the Year

Tony Rose, was born in Roxbury, (Boston) Massachusetts and raised in the Whittier Street Housing Projects. He is an *NAACP Image Award Winner for Outstanding Literature,* the Publisher and CEO of Amber Communications Group, Inc., the nation's largest African American Publisher of Self-Help Books and Music Biographies and the *2013 44th Annual NAACP Image Award Winner for Outstanding Literature* (Youth/Teens) for the title, *Obama Talks Back: Global Lessons – A Dialogue for America's Young Leaders* (Amber Books) by Gregory J. Reed, Esq.

Rose is the editor of numerous books and the co-writer of the national bestseller, *Is Modeling For You? The Handbook and Guide For The Young Aspiring Black Model,* written with Yvonne Rose, and has penned the critically acclaimed, international best-seller, *Before the Legend: The Rise of New Kids On The Block and A Guy Named Maurice Starr, The Early Years.*

He has written, compiled, edited and published, the award winning, international best-seller, *African American History In The United States of America—An Anthology—From Africa To President Barack Obama, Volume One,* a Top Ten Best African American Book and has recently written the critically acclaimed, international best-seller, non-fiction book of the year and a Top Ten Best Black Book of 2015, *America the Black Point of View—An Investigation and Study of the White People of America and Western Europe & The Autobiography of an American Ghetto Boy—The 1950's and 1960's—From the Projects to NAACP Image Award Winner, Volume One.*

And has recently re-vised into a separate book An Investigation and Study of the White People of America and Western Europe and also re-vised into a separate book The Autobiography of an American Ghetto Boy.

WWW.AMBERBOOKS.COM
WWW.QUALITYPRESS.INFO
WWW.AFRICANAMERICANPAVILION.COM
WWW.THEBLACKPOINTOFVIEW.COM

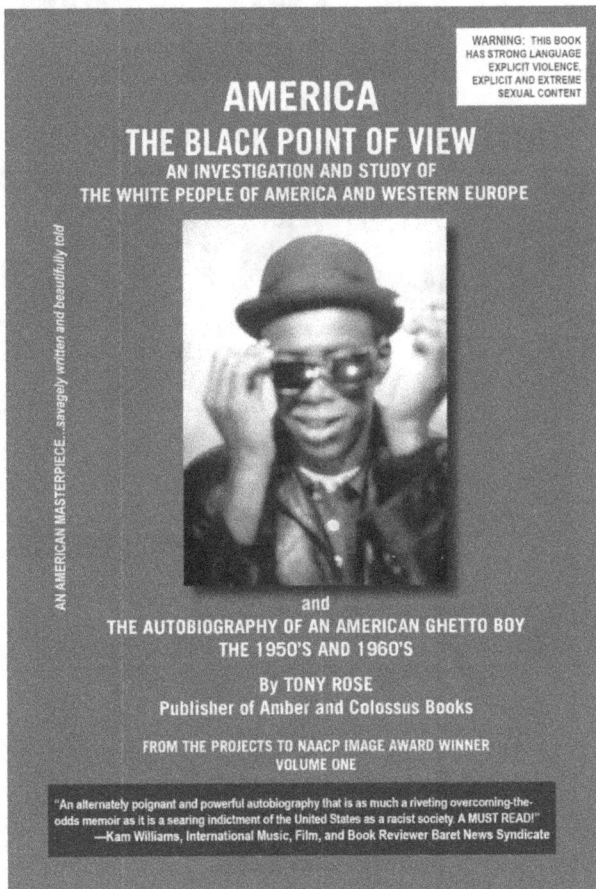

A TOP TEN BEST AFRICAN AMERICAN BOOK

- Kam Williams, International Music, Book and Film Reviewer

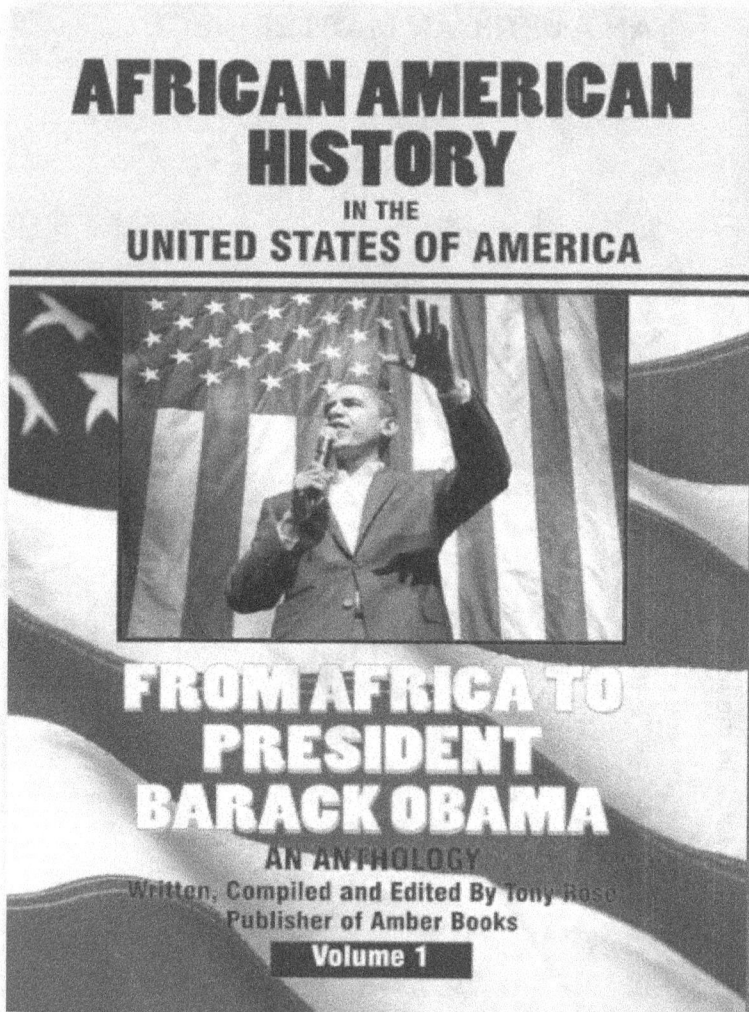

AFRICAN AMERICAN HISTORY
IN THE
UNITED STATES OF AMERICA

FROM AFRICA TO PRESIDENT BARACK OBAMA
AN ANTHOLOGY
Written, Compiled and Edited By Tony Rose
Publisher of Amber Books

Volume 1

AMBER BOOKS
Paperback ISBN #: 978-0-9824922-0-8 - 432 PAGES / $17.95
eBook ISBN #: 978-1-937269-17-3 // $5.00

The history of Africans and African Americans and Europeans and European Americans (Black and White people) in the United States of America

Books are available everywhere and at all on-line and digital sources, including Amazon and BarnesandNoble.com

Contact: amberbk@aol.com for information

WWW.AMBERBOOKS.COM

SLAVERY, SEGREGATION INSTITUTIONAL RACISM

Savagely written

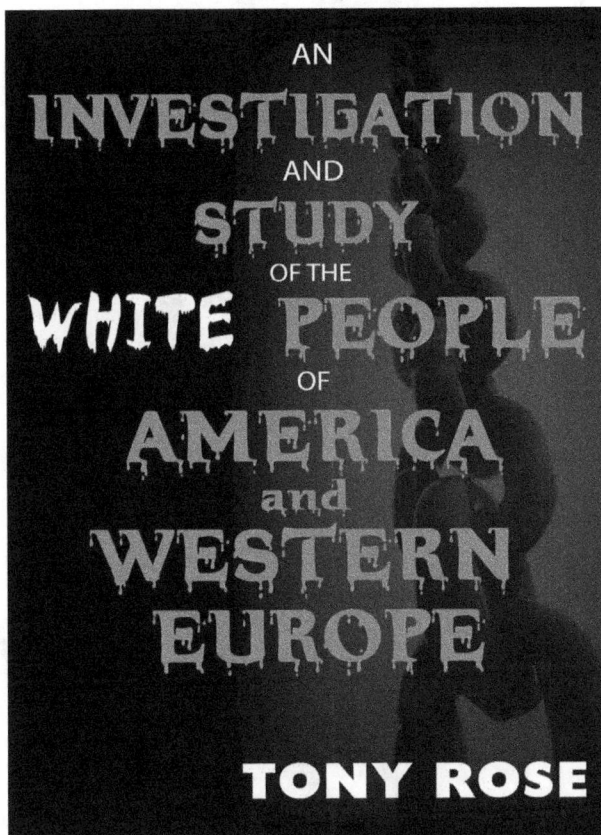

AN

INVESTIGATION

AND

STUDY

OF THE

WHITE PEOPLE

OF

AMERICA

and

WESTERN EUROPE

TONY ROSE

AMBER BOOKS
Paperback ISBN #: 978-1-937269-48-7 / 164 PAGES / / $15.95
eBook ISBN #: 978-1-937269-49-4 // $2.99

Books are available everywhere and at all on-line and digital sources,
including Amazon and BarnesandNoble.com
Contact: amberbk@aol.com for information

WWW.AMBERBOOKS.COM // WWW.THEINVESTIGATIONOFWHITEPEOPLE.COM

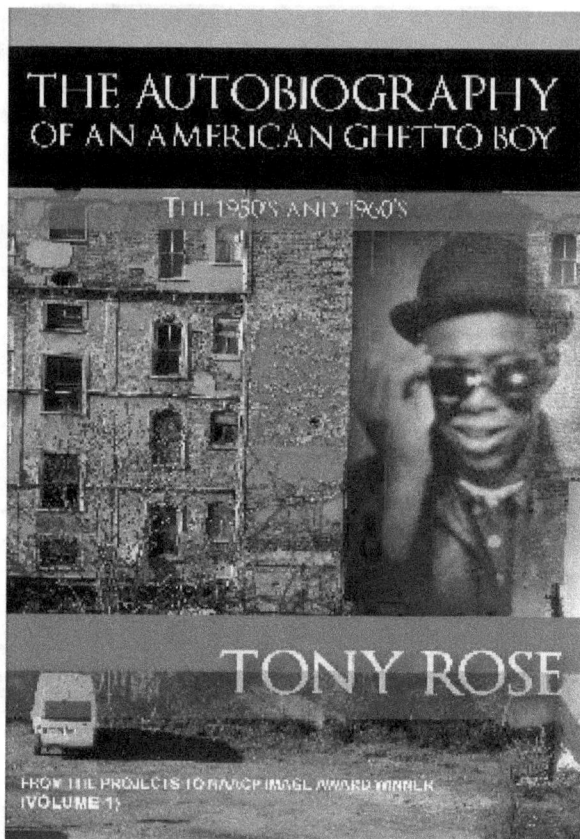

BOOKS BY TONY ROSE

An Investigation and Study of the White People of Western Europe and America
(ISBN # 978-1-937269-48-7)

The Autobiography of an American Ghetto Boy (ISBN # 978-1-937269-52-4)

An Investigation and Study of the White People of Western Europe and America & The Autobiography of an American Ghetto Boy – The 1950's and 1960's -From the Projects to NAACP Image Award Winner, Volume One (ISBN # 978-1-937269-50-0)

African American History In The United States of America - An Anthology - From Africa To President Barack Obama, Volume One (ISBN # 978-0-9824922-0-8)

The Rise of New Kids On The Block and....A Guy Named Maurice Starr, The Early Years (ISBN # 978-0-9790976-7-6)

Is Modeling For You? The Handbook and Guide for the Young Aspiring Black Model (ISBN # 978-0-9790976-9-0)

ORDER FORM

Mail Checks/Money Orders to: Amber Communications Group, Inc.
1334 East Chandler Boulevard – Suite 5-D67, Phoenix, AZ 85048

Please send _____ copy(ies) of *The Autobiography of an American Ghetto Boy* by Tony Rose ($19.95)

Please send _____ copy(ies) of *An Investigation and Study of the White People of America and Western Europe* by Tony Rose ($15.95)

Please send _____ copy(ies) of *America The Black Point of View - An Investigation and Study of the White People of America and Western Europe and The Autobiography of an American Ghetto Boy, The 1950s and 1960s* by Tony Rose ($21.95)

Please send _____ copy(ies) of *African American History in the United States of America from Africa to President Barack Obama* by Tony Rose ($17.95)

Please send _____ copy(ies) of *Obama Talks Back: Global Lessons...A Dialogue for America's Young Leaders* by Gregory J. Reed, Esq. ($19.95)

Please send _____ copy(ies) of *The African American Family's Guide to Tracing Our Roots* by Roland Barksdale Hall ($14.95)

Please send _____ copy(ies) of *African Americans and the Future of New Orleans* by Philip Hart, Ph.D. ($16.95)

Name: _____

Address: _____City: St: Zip: _____

Phone:(   ) _____Email:_____

I have enclosed $_____, plus $5.00 shipping per book for a total of $_____.

For Bulk or Wholesale Rates, Call: 602-743-7211
Or email: Amberbk@aol.com
Please visit: WWW.AMBERBOOKS.COM

www.ingramcontent.com/pod-product-compliance
Lightning Source LLC
Chambersburg PA
CBHW070753290326
41931CB00011BA/1992